OLD-FASHIONED
COOKIES

©Debbie Mumm

Illustrated by
DEBBIE MUMM.

pil

Publications International, Ltd.

Favorite Brand Name Recipes at www.fbnr.com

ISBN: 0-7853-8304-2

Library of Congress Control Number: 2002112010

Manufactured in China.   ₒ

8 7 6 5 4 3 2 1

Microwave Cooking: Microwave ovens vary in wattage. Use the cooking times as guidelines and check for doneness before adding more time.

Preparation/Cooking Times: Preparation times are based on the approximate amount of time required to assemble the recipe before cooking, baking, chilling or serving. These times include preparation steps such as measuring, chopping and mixing. The fact that some preparations and cooking can be done simultaneously is taken into account. Preparation of optional ingredients and serving suggestions is not included.

Contents

Irresistible Peanut Butter Cookies

1¼ cups firmly packed light brown sugar
¾ cup JIF® Creamy Peanut Butter
½ Butter Flavor CRISCO® Stick or ½ cup Butter
　　Flavor CRISCO® all-vegetable shortening
3 tablespoons milk
1 tablespoon vanilla
1 egg
1¾ cups all-purpose flour
¾ teaspoon baking soda
¾ teaspoon salt

1. Heat oven to 375°F. Place sheets of foil on countertop for cooling cookies.

2. Combine brown sugar, peanut butter, shortening, milk and vanilla in large bowl. Beat at medium speed of electric mixer until well blended. Add egg. Beat just until blended.

3. Combine flour, baking soda and salt. Add to creamed mixture at low speed. Mix just until blended.

4. Drop by rounded measuring tablespoonfuls of dough 2 inches apart onto *ungreased* baking sheets. Flatten slightly in crisscross pattern with tines of fork.

5. Bake one baking sheet at a time at 375°F for 7 to 8 minutes or until set and just beginning to brown. *Do not overbake.* Cool 2 minutes on baking sheet. Remove cookies to foil to cool completely. *Makes about 3 dozen cookies*

Almond Cookies

    1 **CRISCO® Stick or 1 cup CRISCO® all-vegetable shortening**
    1 **cup granulated sugar**
    1 **large egg, lightly beaten**
    3 **tablespoons almond extract**
 2¼ **cups all-purpose flour**
 1½ **teaspoons baking powder**
  ¼ **teaspoon salt**
    About 48 whole almonds

1. Combine shortening and sugar in large bowl. Beat at medium speed with electric mixer until well blended. Beat in egg and almond extract.

2. Combine flour, baking powder and salt in medium bowl. Add to creamed mixture; blend well. Wrap dough in plastic wrap and refrigerate 2 hours.

3. Heat oven to 350°F.

4. Roll rounded tablespoonfuls of dough into balls. Place onto *ungreased* cookie sheets about 2 inches apart; flatten slightly with fingertips. Gently press an almond into center of each.

5. Bake at 350°F for 10 to 12 minutes or until cookies are just done but not brown. Cool on cookie sheet 4 minutes; transfer to cooling racks.

Makes about 4 dozen cookies

Ranger Cookies

1 **cup (2 sticks) margarine or butter, softened**
1 **cup granulated sugar**
1 **cup firmly packed brown sugar**
2 **eggs**
1 **teaspoon vanilla**
2 **cups all-purpose flour**
1 **teaspoon baking soda**
½ **teaspoon baking powder**
½ **teaspoon salt (optional)**
2 **cups QUAKER® Oats (quick or old fashioned, uncooked)**
2 **cups cornflakes**
½ **cup flaked or shredded coconut**
½ **cup chopped nuts**

Heat oven to 350°F. Beat margarine and sugars until creamy. Add eggs and vanilla; beat well. Add combined flour, baking soda, baking powder and salt; mix well. Stir in oats, cornflakes, coconut and nuts; mix well. Drop dough by heaping tablespoonfuls onto *ungreased* cookie sheets. Bake 10 to 12 minutes or until light golden brown. Cool 1 minute on cookie sheets; remove to wire rack. Cool completely. Store tightly covered.   *Makes 2 dozen large cookies*

There's no problem that can't be solved with a plate of warm cookies.

Soft Spicy Molasses Cookies

    2 cups all-purpose flour
    1 cup sugar
  ¾ cup (1½ stick) butter, softened
  ⅓ cup light molasses
    3 tablespoons milk
    1 egg
  ½ teaspoon baking soda
  ½ teaspoon ground ginger
  ½ teaspoon ground cinnamon
  ½ teaspoon ground cloves
  ⅛ teaspoon salt
     Sugar for rolling

1. Combine flour, 1 cup sugar, butter, molasses, milk, egg, baking
soda, ginger, cinnamon, cloves and salt in large bowl. Beat at low
speed of electric mixer 2 to 3 minutes or until well blended, scraping
bowl often. Cover; refrigerate until firm enough to handle, at least
4 hours or overnight.

2. Preheat oven to 350°F. Shape rounded teaspoonfuls of dough into
1-inch balls. Roll in sugar. Place 2 inches apart on *ungreased* cookie
sheets. Bake 10 to 12 minutes or until slightly firm to the touch.
Transfer cookies to wire rack. Cool completely.

Makes about 4 dozen cookies

Snickerdoodles

2 cups sugar, divided
1 Butter Flavor CRISCO® Stick or 1 cup Butter Flavor
    CRISCO® all-vegetable shortening
2 eggs
2 tablespoons milk
1 teaspoon vanilla
2¾ cups all-purpose flour
2 teaspoons cream of tartar
1 teaspoon baking soda
¾ teaspoon salt
2 teaspoons ground cinnamon

1. Heat oven to 400°F. Place sheets of foil on countertop for cooling cookies.

2. Combine 1½ cups sugar, shortening, eggs, milk and vanilla in large bowl. Beat at medium speed with electric mixer until well blended.

3. Combine flour, cream of tartar, baking soda and salt. Add gradually to creamed mixture at low speed. Mix just until blended. Shape dough into 1-inch balls.

4. Combine remaining ½ cup sugar and cinnamon in small bowl. Roll balls of dough in mixture. Place 2 inches apart on *ungreased* baking sheet.

5. Bake for 7 to 8 minutes. *Do not overbake.* Cool 2 minutes on baking sheet. Remove cookies to foil to cool completely.

Makes 6 dozen cookies

Cook's Tip: Cinnamon-sugar mixture can be put in resealable plastic bag. Put 2 to 3 dough balls at a time in bag. Seal. Shake to sugar-coat dough.

Colored Sugar Snickerdoodles: Add 2 teaspoons cinnamon to flour mixture in Step 3. Combine 3 tablespoons colored sugar and 3 tablespoons granulated sugar. Use for coating instead of cinnamon-sugar mixture in Step 4.

Smucker's® Grandmother's Jelly Cookies

- 1½ **cups sugar**
- 1 **cup butter or margarine, softened**
- 1 **egg**
- 1½ **teaspoons vanilla extract**
- 3½ **cups all-purpose flour**
- 1 **teaspoon salt**
- ¾ **cup SMUCKER'S® Red Raspberry, Strawberry or Peach Preserves**

In a large bowl, cream together sugar and butter until light and fluffy. Add egg and vanilla; beat well. Stir in flour and salt; mix well. Stir to make a smooth dough. (If batter gets too hard to handle, mix with hands.) Cover and refrigerate about 2 hours.

Preheat oven to 375°F. Lightly grease baking sheets. On lightly floured board, roll out half of dough to about ⅛-inch thickness. Cut out cookies with 2½-inch round cookie cutter. Roll out remaining dough; cut with 2½-inch cutter with hole in center. Place on baking sheets. Bake 8 to 10 minutes or until lightly browned. Cool about 30 minutes.

To serve, spread preserves on plain cookies; top with cookies with holes. *Makes approximately 3 dozen cookies*

Butterscotch Cookies with Burnt Butter Icing

½ **cup butter, softened**
1½ **cups packed brown sugar**
2 **eggs**
1 **teaspoon vanilla**
2½ **cups flour**
1 **teaspoon baking soda**
½ **teaspoon salt**
1 **cup dairy sour cream**
1 **cup finely chopped walnuts**
Burnt Butter Icing (recipe follows)

Beat butter and sugar until light and fluffy. Blend in eggs and vanilla; mix well. Add combined dry ingredients alternately with sour cream, mixing well after each addition. Stir in nuts. Chill 4 hours or over night. Drop rounded teaspoonfuls of dough, 3 inches apart, onto well buttered cookie sheet. Bake at 400°F for 8 to 10 minutes or until lightly browned. Cool. Frost with Burnt Butter Icing.

Makes 5 dozen cookies

Burnt Butter Icing: Melt 6 tablespoons butter in small saucepan over medium heat; continue heating until golden brown. Cool. Blend in 2 cups sifted powdered sugar and 1 teaspoon vanilla. Add 2 to 3 tablespoons water, a little at a time, until spreading consistency is reached.

Favorite recipe from **Wisconsin Milk Marketing Board**

Citrus-Ginger Cookies

1 Butter Flavor CRISCO® Stick or 1 cup Butter Flavor
    CRISCO® all-vegetable shortening
1½ cups granulated sugar
  1 large egg
  2 tablespoons light corn syrup
  1 teaspoon vanilla
  3 cups all-purpose flour
  3 teaspoons ground ginger
  2 teaspoons baking soda
 ½ teaspoon fresh grated orange peel
 ½ teaspoon fresh grated lemon peel
 ½ teaspoon fresh grated lime peel

1. Combine shortening and sugar in large bowl. Beat at medium speed with electric mixer until well blended. Beat in egg, corn syrup and vanilla until well blended.

2. Combine flour, ginger and baking soda in small bowl. Add to creamed mixture. Add orange, lemon and lime peel until well blended.

3. Shape dough into two rolls about 2 inches in diameter. Wrap tightly in plastic wrap; refrigerate 3 hours or overnight.

4. Heat oven to 350°F.

5. Slice dough about ⅛ inch thick. Place 2 inches apart on *ungreased* cookie sheets. Bake at 350°F for 6 to 8 minutes or until lightly brown. Cool on cookie sheets 4 minutes; transfer to cooling racks.

Makes about 7 dozen cookies

Drop Sugar Cookies

2½ **cups sifted all-purpose flour**
½ **teaspoon ARM & HAMMER® Baking Soda**
¼ **teaspoon salt**
½ **cup butter, softened**
½ **cup butter-flavored shortening**
1 **cup sugar**
1 **egg** *or* ¼ **cup egg substitute**
1 **teaspoon vanilla extract**
2 **teaspoons skim milk**

Preheat oven to 400°F. Sift together flour, Baking Soda and salt; set aside. Beat butter and shortening in large bowl with electric mixer on medium speed until blended; add sugar gradually and continue beating until light and fluffy. Beat in egg and vanilla. Add flour mixture and beat until smooth; blend in milk. Drop dough by teaspoonfuls about 3 inches apart onto greased cookie sheets. Flatten with bottom of greased glass that has been dipped in sugar.

Bake 12 minutes or until edges are lightly browned. Cool on wire racks. *Makes about 5½ dozen cookies*

Corn Flake Macaroons

   4 egg whites
  ¼ teaspoon cream of tartar
   1 teaspoon vanilla
 1⅓ cups sugar
   1 cup chopped pecans
   1 cup shredded coconut
   3 cups KELLOGG'S CORN FLAKES® cereal

1. Preheat oven to 325°F. In large bowl, beat egg whites until foamy. Stir in cream of tartar and vanilla. Gradually add sugar, beating until stiff and glossy. Stir in pecans, coconut and Kellogg's Corn Flakes® cereal. Drop by rounded measuring tablespoonfuls onto cookie sheets sprayed with vegetable cooking spray.

2. Bake about 15 minutes or until lightly browned. Remove immediately from cookie sheets. Cool on wire racks.

Makes about 3 dozen cookies

Variation: Fold in ½ cup crushed peppermint candy with pecans and coconut.

Anna's Icing Oatmeal Sandwich Cookies

Cookies
- ¾ **Butter Flavor CRISCO® Stick or ¾ cup Butter Flavor CRISCO® all-vegetable shortening plus additional for greasing**
- 1¼ **cups firmly packed light brown sugar**
- 1 **egg**
- ⅓ **cup milk**
- 1½ **teaspoons vanilla**
- 3 **cups quick oats, uncooked**
- 1 **cup all-purpose flour**
- ½ **teaspoon baking soda**
- ½ **teaspoon salt**

Frosting
- 2 **cups confectioners' sugar**
- ¼ **Butter Flavor CRISCO® Stick or ¼ cup Butter Flavor CRISCO® all-vegetable shortening**
- ½ **teaspoon vanilla**
- **Milk**

1. Heat oven to 350°F. Grease baking sheets with shortening. Place sheets of foil on countertop for cooling cookies.

2. For cookies, combine shortening, brown sugar, egg, milk and vanilla in large bowl. Beat at medium speed of electric mixer until blended.

3. Combine oats, flour, baking soda and salt. Mix into creamed mixture at low speed just until blended. Drop rounded measuring tablespoonfuls of dough 2 inches apart onto prepared baking sheets.

4. Bake one sheet at a time at 375°F for 10 to 12 minutes or until lightly browned. *Do not overbake.* Cool 2 minutes on baking sheet. Remove cookies to foil to cool completely.

5. For frosting, combine confectioners' sugar, shortening and vanilla. Beat at low speed, adding enough milk for good spreading consistency. Spread on bottoms of half the cookies. Top with remaining cookies. *Makes about 16 sandwich cookies*

Domino® Sugar Cookies

1 cup DOMINO® Granulated Sugar
1 cup (2 sticks) butter or margarine, softened
1 egg
1 tablespoon vanilla
2¼ cups all-purpose flour
1 teaspoon baking soda
Additional DOMINO® Granulated Sugar

In large bowl, blend sugar and butter. Beat in egg and vanilla until light and fluffy. Mix in flour and baking soda. Divide dough in half. Shape each half into roll about 1½ inches in diameter. Wrap and refrigerate for 1 hour until chilled.* Cut rolls into ¼-inch slices. Place on *ungreased* baking sheet and sprinkle generously with additional sugar. Bake in 375°F oven 10 to 12 minutes or until lightly browned around edges. Cool on wire rack.

Makes about 3 dozen cookies

* To chill dough quickly, place in freezer for 30 minutes.

Date-Nut Macaroons

1 (8-ounce) package pitted dates, chopped
1½ cups BAKER'S® Angel Flake Coconut
1 cup PLANTERS® Pecan Halves, chopped
¾ cup sweetened condensed milk (not evaporated milk)
½ teaspoon vanilla extract

Preheat oven to 350°F.

Combine dates, coconut and nuts in medium bowl; blend in sweetened condensed milk and vanilla. Drop by rounded tablespoonfuls onto greased and floured cookie sheets. Bake 10 to 12 minutes or until light golden brown. Carefully remove from cookie sheets; cool completely on wire racks. Store in airtight container.

Makes about 2 dozen cookies

Double Lemon Delights

2¼ **cups all-purpose flour**
½ **teaspoon baking powder**
½ **teaspoon salt**
1 **cup (2 sticks) butter, softened**
¾ **cup granulated sugar**
1 **egg**
2 **tablespoons grated lemon peel, divided**
1 **teaspoon vanilla**
Additional sugar
1 **cup powdered sugar**
4 **to 5 teaspoons lemon juice**

1. Preheat oven to 375°F.

2. Combine flour, baking powder and salt in small bowl; set aside. Beat butter and granulated sugar in large bowl with electric mixer at medium speed until light and fluffy. Beat in egg, 1 tablespoon lemon peel and vanilla until well blended. Gradually beat in flour mixture on low speed until blended.

3. Drop dough by level ¼ cupfuls onto *ungreased* cookie sheets, spacing 3 inches apart. Flatten dough until 3 inches in diameter with bottom of glass that has been dipped in additional sugar.

4. Bake 12 to 14 minutes or until cookies are just set and edges are golden brown. Cool on cookie sheets 2 minutes; transfer to wire racks. Cool completely.

5. Combine powdered sugar, lemon juice and remaining 1 tablespoon lemon peel in small bowl; drizzle mixture over cookies. Let stand until icing is set.

Makes about 1 dozen (4-inch) cookies

Date-Oatmeal Cookies

Prep Time: 15 minutes
Bake Time: 12 minutes

- **1 cup all-purpose flour**
- **¾ cup quick-cooking oats**
- **1 cup DOLE® Chopped Dates or Pitted Prunes, chopped**
- **1 teaspoon ground cinnamon**
- **¾ teaspoon baking powder**
- **⅔ cup packed brown sugar**
- **1 medium ripe DOLE® Banana, mashed (½ cup)**
- **¼ cup margarine, softened**
- **1 egg**
- **1 teaspoon vanilla extract**
- **Vegetable cooking spray**

• Combine flour, oats, dates, cinnamon and baking powder in bowl; set aside.

• Beat together sugar, banana, margarine, egg and vanilla until well blended. Add flour mixture; stir until ingredients are moistened.

• Drop dough by rounded teaspoonfuls, 2 inches apart, onto baking sheets sprayed with vegetable cooking spray.

• Bake at 375°F 10 to 12 minutes or until lightly brown. Remove cookies to wire rack; cool. Store in airtight container.

Makes 32 cookies

Frosted Pumpkin Softies

Cookies
- 1 cup (2 sticks) margarine or butter, softened
- ¾ cup granulated sugar
- ¾ cup firmly packed brown sugar
- 1 cup canned pumpkin
- 1 egg
- 1 teaspoon vanilla
- 2½ cups QUAKER® Oats (quick or old fashioned, uncooked)
- 1¾ cups all-purpose flour
- 1 teaspoon baking soda
- 1 teaspoon pumpkin pie spice or ground cinnamon
- ¼ teaspoon salt (optional)

Frosting
- 3 ounces cream cheese, softened
- 1 tablespoon milk
- ½ teaspoon vanilla
- 2½ cups powdered sugar
- Yellow and red food coloring (optional)

Heat oven to 350°F. Beat together margarine and sugars until creamy. Add pumpkin, egg and vanilla; beat well. Add combined oats, flour, baking soda, pumpkin pie spice and salt, if desired; mix well. Drop by rounded tablespoonfuls onto *ungreased* cookie sheets. Bake 11 to 13 minutes or until light golden brown. Cool 1 minute on cookie sheets; remove to wire rack. Cool completely.

For frosting, beat together cream cheese, milk and vanilla until smooth. Gradually beat in powdered sugar until smooth; tint with food color, if desired. Frost top of each cookie. Store in tightly covered container in refrigerator. *Makes about 4 dozen*

Gingersnaps

2½ cups all-purpose flour
1½ teaspoons ground ginger
1 teaspoon baking soda
1 teaspoon ground allspice
½ teaspoon salt
1½ cups sugar
2 tablespoons margarine, softened
½ cup MOTT'S® Apple Sauce
¼ cup GRANDMA'S® Molasses

1. Preheat oven to 375°F. Spray cookie sheet with nonstick cooking spray.

2. In medium bowl, sift together flour, ginger, baking soda, allspice and salt.

3. In large bowl, beat sugar and margarine with electric mixer at medium speed until blended. Whisk in apple sauce and molasses.

4. Add flour mixture to apple sauce mixture; stir until well blended.

5. Drop rounded tablespoonfuls of dough 1 inch apart onto prepared cookie sheet. Flatten each slightly with moistened fingertips.

6. Bake 12 to 15 minutes or until firm. Cool completely on wire rack.

Makes 3 dozen cookies

Hermits

¾ **Butter Flavor CRISCO® Stick or ¾ cup Butter Flavor CRISCO® all-vegetable shortening**
1½ **cups firmly packed brown sugar**
2 **tablespoons milk**
3 **eggs**
2½ **cups all-purpose flour**
1 **teaspoon salt**
1 **teaspoon cinnamon**
¾ **teaspoon baking soda**
¼ **teaspoon nutmeg**
⅛ **teaspoon ground cloves**
1 **cup raisins**
¾ **cup chopped walnuts**
Powdered sugar

1. Heat oven to 400°F. Place sheets of foil on countertop for cooling cookies.

2. Combine shortening, sugar and milk in large bowl. Beat at medium speed of electric mixer until well blended. Add eggs one at a time. Beat well after each addition.

3. Combine flour, salt, cinnamon, baking soda, nutmeg and cloves. Mix into creamed mixture at low speed just until blended. Stir in raisins and nuts.

4. Drop level tablespoonfuls of dough 2 inches apart onto *ungreased* baking sheet.

5. Bake at 400°F for 7 to 8 minutes or until set. *Do not overbake.* Remove cookies to foil to cool completely. Sift powdered sugar over cooled cookies.   *Makes about 5 dozen cookies*

Molasses Oatmeal Cookies

1 **Butter Flavor CRISCO® Stick or 1 cup Butter Flavor CRISCO® all-vegetable shortening plus additional for greasing**
1 **cup granulated sugar**
1 **cup firmly packed brown sugar**
2 **eggs**
1 **tablespoon milk**
1 **tablespoon light molasses**
2 **teaspoons vanilla**
2 **cups all-purpose flour**
1½ **teaspoons cinnamon**
1 **teaspoon baking soda**
½ **teaspoon baking powder**
½ **teaspoon ground cloves**
¼ **teaspoon salt**
2 **cups quick oats (not instant or old fashioned)**
1 **cup coarsely chopped pecans**
½ **cup raisins**

1. Heat oven to 350°F. Grease baking sheets with shortening. Place sheets of foil on countertop for cooling cookies.

2. Combine shortening, granulated sugar, brown sugar, eggs, milk, molasses and vanilla in large bowl. Beat at medium speed of electric mixer until well blended.

3. Combine flour, cinnamon, baking soda, baking powder, cloves and salt. Stir into creamed mixture with spoon until well blended. Stir in oats, nuts and raisins.

4. Form dough into 1-inch balls. Place 2 inches apart on baking sheet.

5. Bake at 350°F for 11 to 12 minutes or until edges are lightly browned. *Do not overbake.* Cool 2 minutes on baking sheet. Remove cookies to foil to cool completely.   *Makes about 4 dozen cookies*

Basic Icebox Cookie Dough

1 cup butter or margarine, softened
1 cup sugar
1 egg
1 teaspoon vanilla
2½ cups all-purpose flour
1 teaspoon baking powder
½ teaspoon salt

Beat butter and sugar with an electric mixer. Add egg and vanilla; mix well. Combine flour, baking powder and salt. Gradually add to butter mixture; mix well.   *Makes 4½ cups dough*

Maraschino Cherry Cookies: Add ½ cup chopped well-drained maraschino cherries to basic dough; divide dough in half. Form dough into 2 logs, 1½ inches in diameter. Wrap in waxed paper and refrigerate at least 6 hours. Cut into ¼-inch slices. Place on *ungreased* baking sheets. Bake at 375°F 8 to 10 minutes. Remove to cooling rack. Repeat with remaining dough. Makes 6 to 7 dozen cookies.

Maraschino Date Pinwheels: Combine 8 ounces cut-up pitted dates and ¼ cup water in small saucepan; bring to a boil. Reduce heat; simmer until thickened. Add ¾ cup chopped drained maraschino cherries; mix well and cool. Divide dough in half. Roll out each half to 12×10-inch rectangle on lightly floured surface. Spread half of cooled filling on each rectangle. Roll up beginning at long ends. Pinch ends of rolls to seal. Wrap in waxed paper and refrigerate at least 6 hours. Cut rolls into ¼-inch slices. Place 1 to 1½ inches apart on *ungreased* baking sheet. Bake at 375°F about 10 to 14 minutes or until lightly browned. Remove to cooling rack. Makes 6 to 7 dozen cookies.

Maraschino Thumbprint Cookies: Shape dough into balls, using 2 teaspoons dough for each cookie. Press thumb in center of each ball. Place whole well-drained maraschino cherry in center of each depression. Brush with beaten egg white. If desired, roll each ball in beaten egg white, then in finely chopped pecans before pressing with thumb and filling with cherry. Bake at 375°F 12 to 15 minutes. Remove to cooling rack. Makes 5 dozen cookies.

Favorite recipes from **Cherry Marketing Institute**

Honey Ginger Snaps

    2 cups all-purpose flour
    1 tablespoon ground ginger
    2 teaspoons baking soda
    ⅛ teaspoon salt
    ⅛ teaspoon ground cloves
    ½ cup shortening
    ¼ cup (½ stick) butter, softened
  1½ cups sugar, divided
    ¼ cup honey
    1 egg
    1 teaspoon vanilla

1. Preheat oven to 350°F. Grease cookie sheets. Combine flour, ginger, baking soda, salt and cloves in medium bowl.

2. Beat shortening and butter in large bowl with electric mixer at medium speed until smooth. Gradually beat in 1 cup sugar until blended; increase speed to high and beat until light and fluffy. Beat in honey, egg and vanilla until fluffy. Gradually stir in flour mixture until blended.

3. Shape mixture into 1-inch balls. Place remaining ½ cup sugar in shallow bowl; roll balls in sugar to coat. Place 2 inches apart on prepared cookie sheets.

4. Bake 10 minutes or until golden brown. Let cookies stand on cookie sheets 5 minutes; transfer to wire racks to cool completely. Store in airtight container up to 1 week.   *Makes 3½ dozen cookies*

Favorite Lemon Cookies

- **2 cups all-purpose flour**
- **½ teaspoon baking soda**
- **¼ teaspoon salt**
- **1 cup sugar**
- **⅓ cup butter or margarine, softened**
- **1 egg**
- **Grated peel and juice of 1 SUNKIST® lemon (3 tablespoons juice)**
- **Lemon Frosting (recipe follows) or decorating icing***

*Decorating icing comes in tubes in assorted colors.

Sift together flour, baking soda and salt. In large bowl, cream together sugar and butter. Add egg, lemon peel and juice; beat well. Gradually blend in dry ingredients. Divide dough into 4 parts; cover and chill 1 hour or longer. On lightly floured board, roll ¼ of dough at a time to ⅛-inch thickness. Cut with lightly floured cookie cutters and place on well-greased cookie sheets. Bake at 375°F 10 minutes or until lightly browned. Remove and cool on wire racks. Spread cookies with Lemon Frosting or decorating icing.

Makes about 4 to 5 dozen cookies

Lemon Frosting

- **3 cups confectioners' sugar, divided**
- **⅓ cup butter or margarine, softened, divided**
- **Grated peel of ½ SUNKIST® lemon**
- **2 to 3 tablespoons fresh squeezed SUNKIST® lemon juice**

In bowl, cream together 1 cup sugar and butter. Add remaining 2 cups sugar, lemon peel and juice; mix until smooth. To prevent frosting from drying out too quickly, cover with damp cloth while frosting cookies.

Makes about 1⅓ cups

Oatmeal Apple Cookies

1¼ cups firmly packed brown sugar
¾ Butter Flavor CRISCO® Stick or ¾ cup Butter Flavor
    CRISCO® all-vegetable shortening plus additional
    for greasing
¼ cup milk
1 egg
1½ teaspoons vanilla
1 cup all-purpose flour
1¼ teaspoons ground cinnamon
½ teaspoon salt
¼ teaspoon baking soda
¼ teaspoon ground nutmeg
3 cups quick oats (not instant or old-fashioned), uncooked
1 cup diced peeled apples
¾ cup raisins (optional)
¾ cup coarsely chopped walnuts (optional)

1. Heat oven to 375°F. Grease baking sheets. Place sheets of foil on countertop for cooling cookies.

2. Combine brown sugar, shortening, milk, egg and vanilla in large bowl. Beat at medium speed of electric mixer until well blended and creamy.

3. Combine flour, cinnamon, salt, baking soda and nutmeg. Add gradually to creamed mixture at low speed. Mix just until blended. Stir in, one at a time, oats, apples, raisins and nuts, if desired, with spoon. Drop by rounded tablespoonfuls 2 inches apart onto prepared baking sheet.

4. Bake at 375°F for 13 minutes or until set. *Do not overbake.* Cool 2 minutes on baking sheet. Remove cookies to foil to cool completely.

Makes about 2½ dozen cookies

Coconut Cream Cheese Cookies

1 **Butter Flavor CRISCO® Stick or 1 cup Butter Flavor CRISCO® all-vegetable shortening**
6 **ounces cream cheese, softened**
1 **cup granulated sugar**
1 **teaspoon almond extract**
1 **teaspoon vanilla**
¼ **teaspoon salt**
1 **large egg**
2 **tablespoons milk**
2 **cups all-purpose flour**
½ **cup toasted flaked coconut**

1. Heat oven to 325°F.

2. Combine shortening, cream cheese, sugar, almond extract, vanilla and salt in large bowl. Beat at medium speed with electric mixer until well blended. Beat in egg and milk until well blended. Add flour and coconut; mix well.

3. Drop rounded teaspoonfuls of dough about 2 inches apart onto *ungreased* cookie sheets.

4. Bake at 325°F for 15 to 20 minutes until lightly browned. Cool on cookie sheets 4 minutes; transfer to cooling racks.

Makes about 5 dozen cookies

Old-Fashioned Harvest Cookies

¾ **Butter Flavor CRISCO® Stick or ¾ cup Butter Flavor CRISCO® all-vegetable shortening**
1 **cup firmly packed dark brown sugar**
¾ **cup canned solid-pack pumpkin**
1 **egg**
2 **tablespoons molasses**
1½ **cups all-purpose flour**
1 **teaspoon ground nutmeg**
½ **teaspoon baking powder**
½ **teaspoon baking soda**
¼ **teaspoon salt**
¼ **teaspoon ground cinnamon**
2½ **cups quick oats (not instant or old-fashioned), uncooked**
1½ **cups finely chopped dates**
½ **cup chopped walnuts**

1. Heat oven to 350°F. Grease baking sheets. Place sheets of foil on countertop for cooling cookies.

2. Combine shortening and sugar in large bowl. Beat at medium speed of electric mixer until well blended. Beat in pumpkin, egg and molasses.

3. Combine flour, nutmeg, baking powder, baking soda, salt and cinnamon. Mix into creamed mixture at low speed until just blended. Stir in, one a time, oats, dates and nuts with spoon.

4. Drop rounded tablespoonfuls of dough 2 inches apart onto cookie sheet.

5. Bake at 350°F for 10 to 12 minutes or until bottoms are lightly browned. *Do not overbake.* Cool 2 minutes on baking sheet. Remove cookies to foil to cool completely.   *Makes about 4 dozen cookies*

Oatmeal Hermits

3 cups QUAKER® Oats (quick or old fashioned, uncooked)
1 cup all-purpose flour
1 cup firmly packed brown sugar
1 cup (2 sticks) butter or margarine, melted
1 cup raisins
½ cup chopped nuts
1 egg
¼ cup milk
1 teaspoon ground cinnamon
1 teaspoon vanilla
½ teaspoon baking soda
½ teaspoon salt (optional)
¼ teaspoon ground nutmeg

Heat oven to 375°F. In large bowl, combine all ingredients; mix well.
Drop by rounded tablespoonfuls onto *ungreased* cookie sheets. Bake
8 to 10 minutes. Cool 1 minute on cookie sheets; remove to wire
cooling rack.   *Makes about 3 dozen*

For Bar Cookies: Press dough into *ungreased* 15×10-inch jelly-roll pan.
Bake about 17 minutes or until golden brown. Cool completely; cut
into bars.

Home is where you can put your feet up and let your guard down.

P.B. & J. Cookies

1½ **cups sugar**
1 **Butter Flavor CRISCO® Stick or 1 cup Butter Flavor CRISCO® all-vegetable shortening plus additional for greasing**
1 **cup JIF® Creamy Peanut Butter**
3 **eggs**
3 **cups all-purpose flour**
1 **tablespoon cream of tartar**
1 **teaspoon baking soda**
½ **teaspoon salt**
2 **cups slightly crushed crisp rice cereal SMUCKER'S® Strawberry Preserves or Jam (or flavor of your choice)***

If desired, top with additional preserves or jam before serving.

1. Heat oven to 375°F. Grease baking sheets with shortening. Place sheets of foil on countertop for cooling cookies.

2. Combine sugar and shortening in large bowl. Beat at medium speed of electric mixer until well blended. Beat in peanut butter and eggs.

3. Combine flour, cream of tartar, baking soda and salt. Add gradually to creamed mixture at low speed. Beat until well blended. Shape dough into 1¼-inch balls. Roll in cereal. Place 2 inches apart on greased baking sheet.

4. Press tip of little finger halfway down in center of ball (don't flatten). Fill hole with about ½ measuring teaspoonful of preserves.

5. Bake at 375°F for 9 to 11 minutes or until light brown. *Do not overbake.* Cool 3 minutes on baking sheet. Remove cookies to foil to cool completely.   *Makes about 4½ dozen cookies*

Old-Fashioned Oatmeal Cookies

¾ **Butter Flavor CRISCO® Stick or ¾ cup Butter Flavor CRISCO® all-vegetable shortening plus additional for greasing**
1¼ **cups firmly packed brown sugar**
1 **egg**
⅓ **cup milk**
1½ **teaspoons vanilla**
3 **cups quick oats, uncooked**
1 **cup all-purpose flour**
½ **teaspoon baking soda**
½ **teaspoon salt**
¼ **teaspoon ground cinnamon**
1 **cup raisins**
1 **cup coarsely chopped walnuts**

1. Heat oven to 375°F. Grease baking sheets with shortening. Place sheets of foil on countertop for cooling cookies.

2. Combine shortening, brown sugar, egg, milk and vanilla in large bowl. Beat at medium speed of electric mixer until well blended.

3. Combine oats, flour, baking soda, salt and cinnamon. Mix into shortening mixture at low speed just until blended. Stir in raisins and walnuts.

4. Drop by rounded measuring tablespoonfuls of dough 2 inches apart onto prepared baking sheets.

5. Bake one baking sheet at a time at 375°F for 10 to 12 minutes or until lightly browned. *Do not overbake.* Cool 2 minutes on baking sheets. Remove cookies to foil to cool completely.

Makes about 2½ dozen cookies

Peanut Butter and Jelly Thumbprints

1½ cups all-purpose flour
½ cup sugar
½ teaspoon baking soda
¼ teaspoon salt
¾ cup PETER PAN® Creamy Peanut Butter
¼ cup butter, softened
¼ cup honey
1 tablespoon milk
   KNOTT'S BERRY FARM® Grape Jelly or any
   favorite flavor

In large bowl, combine flour, sugar, baking soda and salt. Add peanut butter and butter; mix until crumbly. Stir in honey and milk. Shape into 1-inch balls. Place 2 inches apart on *ungreased* baking sheets. Press thumb into center of each ball; place *½ teaspoon* jelly in each thumbprint. Bake at 375°F for 8 to 10 minutes. Cool on baking sheets 1 minute before removing to wire racks. Store in airtight container.

Makes 2 dozen cookies

Maple Walnut Cookies

1¼ cups firmly packed light brown sugar
¾ Butter Flavor CRISCO® Stick or ¾ cup Butter Flavor
    CRISCO® all-vegetable shortening
2 tablespoons maple syrup
1 teaspoon vanilla
1 teaspoon maple extract
1 egg
1¾ cups all-purpose flour
1 teaspoon salt
¾ teaspoon baking soda
½ teaspoon cinnamon
1½ cups chopped walnuts
30 to 40 walnut halves

1. Heat oven to 375°F. Place sheets of foil on countertop for cooling cookies.

2. Place brown sugar, shortening, maple syrup, vanilla and maple extract in large bowl. Beat at medium speed of electric mixer until well blended. Add egg; beat well.

3. Combine flour, salt, baking soda and cinnamon. Add to shortening mixture; beat at low speed just until blended. Stir in chopped walnuts.

4. Drop dough by rounded measuring tablespoonfuls 3 inch apart onto *ungreased* baking sheets. Press walnut half into center of each cookie.

5. Bake one baking sheet at a time at 375°F for 8 to 10 minutes for chewy cookies or 11 to 13 for crisp cookies. *Do not overbake.* Cool 2 minutes on baking sheet. Remove cookies to foil to cool completely.

Makes about 3 dozen cookies

Fresh Orange Cookies

1½ cups all-purpose flour
½ teaspoon baking soda
¼ teaspoon salt
½ cup butter or margarine, softened
½ cup granulated sugar
½ cup packed light brown sugar
1 egg
1 unpeeled SUNKIST® orange, finely chopped*
½ cup chopped walnuts
Orange Glaze (recipe follows)

Chop SUNKIST® orange in blender or food processor, or by hand, to equal ¾ cup chopped fruit.

Sift together flour, baking soda and salt. In large bowl, beat butter and sugars until light and fluffy. Add egg and chopped orange; beat well. Gradually blend in dry ingredients. Stir in walnuts. Cover and chill at least 1 hour. Drop dough by teaspoons onto lightly greased cookie sheets. Bake at 375°F for 10 to 12 minutes. Cool on wire racks. Spread cookies with Orange Glaze.   *Makes about 4 dozen cookies*

Orange Glaze

1 cup confectioners' sugar
1 to 2 tablespoons fresh SUNKIST® orange juice
1 tablespoon butter or margarine, softened
1 teaspoon grated SUNKIST® orange peel

In small bowl, combine all ingredients until smooth.

Makes about ½ cup

Soft Molasses Spice Cookies

2¼ cups all-purpose flour
  1 teaspoon baking soda
  1 teaspoon ground cinnamon
  ½ teaspoon ground ginger
  ¼ teaspoon ground nutmeg
  ⅛ teaspoon salt
  ⅛ teaspoon ground cloves
  ½ cup plus 2 tablespoons butter, softened and divided
  ½ cup packed dark brown sugar
  1 egg
  ½ cup molasses
1¼ teaspoons vanilla, divided
  ¼ cup plus 2 to 3 tablespoons milk, divided
  ¾ cup raisins (optional)
  2 cups powdered sugar

1. Preheat oven to 350°F. Grease cookie sheets. Combine flour, baking soda, cinnamon, ginger, nutmeg, salt and cloves in medium bowl.

2. Beat ½ cup butter in large bowl with electric mixer at medium speed until smooth and creamy. Gradually beat in brown sugar until blended; increase speed to high and beat until light and fluffy. Beat in egg until fluffy. Beat in molasses and 1 teaspoon vanilla until smooth. Beat in flour mixture at low speed alternately with ¼ cup milk until blended. Stir in raisins, if desired.

3. Drop rounded tablespoonfuls of dough about 1½ inches apart onto prepared cookie sheets. Bake 12 minutes or until set. Let cookies stand on cookie sheets 5 minutes; transfer to wire racks to cool completely.

4. For icing, melt remaining 2 tablespoons butter in small saucepan over medium-low heat. Remove from heat; add powdered sugar and stir until blended. Add remaining 2 tablespoons milk and ¼ teaspoon vanilla; stir until smooth. If icing is too thick, add milk, 1 teaspoon at a time, until desired consistency.

5. Spread icing over tops of cookies. Let stand 15 minutes or until icing is set. Store in airtight container. *Makes about 3 dozen cookies*

Applesauce Raisin Chews

1 cup (2 sticks) margarine or butter, softened
1 cup firmly packed brown sugar
1 cup applesauce
1 egg
1 teaspoon vanilla
2 cups all-purpose flour
1 teaspoon baking soda
1 teaspoon ground cinnamon
½ teaspoon salt (optional)
2½ cups QUAKER® Oats (quick or old fashioned, uncooked)
1 cup raisins

Heat oven to 350°F. Beat together margarine and sugar until creamy.
Add applesauce, egg and vanilla; beat well. Add combined flour,
baking soda, cinnamon and salt; mix well. Stir in oats and raisins.
Drop by rounded tablespoonfuls onto *ungreased* cookie sheets. Bake
11 to 13 minutes or until light golden brown. Cool 1 minute on cookie
sheets; remove to wire rack. Cool completely. Store in tightly covered
container.   *Makes about 4 dozen*

Butterscotch Crispies

　　2 cups sifted all-purpose flour
　　1 teaspoon baking soda
　　1 teaspoon salt
　½ cup margarine
2½ cups packed light brown sugar
　　2 eggs
　　1 teaspoon vanilla
　　2 cups quick-cooking rolled oats
　　2 cups puffed rice cereal
　½ cup chopped walnuts

Preheat oven to 350°F. Sift flour, baking soda and salt onto waxed paper. Cream margarine and brown sugar with electric mixer at medium speed in large bowl until fluffy. Beat in eggs, 1 at a time, until fluffy. Stir in vanilla.

Add flour mixture, ⅓ at a time, until well blended; stir in rolled oats, rice cereal and walnuts. Drop by teaspoonfuls, about 1 inch apart, onto large cookie sheets lightly sprayed with nonstick cooking spray. Bake 10 minutes or until cookies are firm and lightly golden. Remove to wire racks; cool. *Makes 8½ dozen cookies*

Favorite recipe from **The Sugar Association, Inc.**

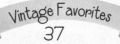

Molasses Spice Cookies

   1 cup granulated sugar
   ¾ cup shortening
   ¼ cup molasses
   1 large egg, beaten
   2 cups all-purpose flour
   2 teaspoons baking soda
   1 teaspoon ground cinnamon
   1 teaspoon ground cloves
   1 teaspoon ground ginger
   ¼ teaspoon salt
   ¼ teaspoon dry mustard
   ½ cup granulated brown sugar or granulated sugar

1. Preheat oven to 375°F. Grease cookie sheets; set aside.

2. Beat granulated sugar and shortening about 5 minutes in large bowl until light and fluffy. Add molasses and egg; beat until fluffy.

3. Combine flour, baking soda, cinnamon, cloves, ginger, salt and mustard in medium bowl. Add to shortening mixture; mix until just combined.

4. Place brown sugar in shallow dish. Roll tablespoonfuls of dough into 1-inch balls; roll in sugar to coat. Place 2 inches apart on prepared cookie sheets. Bake 15 minutes or until lightly browned. Let cookies stand on cookie sheets 2 minutes. Remove cookies to wire racks; cool completely. *Makes about 6 dozen cookies*

Baker's® One Bowl Coconut Macaroons

Prep Time: 15 minutes

> **1 package (14 ounces) BAKER'S® ANGEL FLAKE® Coconut (5⅓ cups)**
> **⅔ cup sugar**
> **6 tablespoons flour**
> **¼ teaspoon salt**
> **4 egg whites**
> **1 teaspoon almond extract**
> **Marachino cherries (optional)**
> **Whole almonds (optional)**

HEAT oven to 325°F.

MIX coconut, sugar, flour and salt in large bowl. Stir in egg whites and almond extract until well blended.

DROP by teaspoonfuls onto greased and floured cookie sheets. Press 1 whole candied cherry or whole natural almond into center of each cookie, if desired.

BAKE 20 minutes or until edges of cookies are golden brown. Immediately remove from cookie sheets. Cool on wire racks.

Makes about 3 dozen cookies

Chocolate Dipped Macaroons: Prepare Coconut Macaroons as directed. Cool. Melt 1 package (8 squares) Baker's® Semi-Sweet Baking Chocolate as directed on package. Dip cookies halfway into chocolate or drizzle tops of cookies with chocolate; let excess chocolate drip off. Let stand at room temperature or refrigerate on wax paper-lined tray 30 minutes or until chocolate is firm.

Chocolate Macaroons: Prepare Coconut Macaroons as directed, adding 2 squares Baker's® Semi-Sweet Baking Chocolate, melted, to mixture.

Bran Fruit and Nut Cookies

Prep Time: 15 minutes
Bake Time: 10 minutes

½ cup firmly packed brown sugar
¼ cup oil
2 egg whites, slightly beaten
2 tablespoons water
1 teaspoon ground cinnamon
½ teaspoon baking soda
⅛ teaspoon salt
1 cup flour
1½ cups POST® Raisin Bran Cereal
¼ cup chopped walnuts
¼ cup chopped dried apricots (optional)

MIX sugar, oil, egg whites, water, cinnamon, baking soda and salt in large bowl. Stir in flour and cereal. Mix in walnuts and apricots, if desired.

DROP by rounded teaspoons onto lightly greased cookie sheets.

BAKE at 350°F for 10 minutes or until browned. Remove and cool on wire racks. Store in tightly covered container.

Makes 4 dozen cookies

Oatmeal Pecan Scotchies

½ **cup margarine or butter, softened**
½ **cup packed light brown sugar**
  1 **egg**
1¼ **cups all-purpose flour**
  1 **cup old-fashioned rolled oats**
  1 **teaspoon CALUMET® Baking Powder**
¼ **cup milk**
½ **cup PLANTERS® Pecan Pieces**
½ **cup butterscotch chips**

1. Beat margarine or butter and sugar in large bowl with mixer at medium speed until creamy. Blend in egg.

2. Mix flour, oats and baking powder in small bowl. Alternately stir flour mixture and milk into egg mixture. Stir in pecans and butterscotch chips.

3. Drop batter by rounded teaspoonfuls onto *ungreased* baking sheets. Bake at 350°F for 12 to 15 minutes or until lightly golden. Remove from pan; cool on wire rack. Store in airtight container.

Makes 4 dozen cookies

Best-Loved Chips

Walnut-Orange Chocolate Chippers

1½ cups all-purpose flour
½ cup granulated sugar
½ cup packed brown sugar
1½ teaspoons baking powder
½ teaspoon salt
⅓ cup butter, softened
2 eggs, slightly beaten
2 cups (12 ounces) semisweet chocolate chips
1 cup coarsely chopped California walnuts
2 tablespoons grated orange rind

Combine flour, granulated sugar, brown sugar, baking powder and salt in large bowl; mix in butter and eggs. Add remaining ingredients and mix thoroughly (batter will be stiff). Drop tablespoonfuls of dough 2 inches apart onto *ungreased* cookies sheets. Bake in preheated 350°F oven 9 to 11 minutes or until lightly browned. Cool 1 minute on cookie sheets; transfer to wire racks to cool completely.

Makes about 3½ dozen cookies

Variation: Prepare dough as directed above. Spread evenly into greased and floured 9-inch square pan (use wet hands to smooth). Bake at 350°F 25 minutes or until golden brown. Cool; cut into 36 squares.

Favorite recipe from **Walnut Marketing Board**

Chewy Brownie Cookies

1½ **cups firmly packed light brown sugar**
⅔ **CRISCO® Stick or ⅔ cup CRISCO® all-vegetable shortening**
1 **tablespoon water**
1 **teaspoon vanilla**
2 **eggs**
1½ **cups all-purpose flour**
⅓ **cup unsweetened baking cocoa**
½ **teaspoon salt**
¼ **teaspoon baking soda**
2 **cups (12-ounce package) semi-sweet chocolate chips**

1. Heat oven to 375°F. Place sheets of foil on countertop for cooling cookies.

2. Combine brown sugar, shortening, water and vanilla in large bowl. Beat at medium speed of electric mixer until well blended. Beat eggs into creamed mixture.

3. Combine flour, cocoa, salt and baking soda. Mix into creamed mixture at low speed just until blended. Stir in chocolate chips.

4. Drop rounded measuring tablespoonfuls of dough 2 inches apart onto *ungreased* baking sheet.

5. Bake one baking sheet at a time at 375°F for 7 to 9 minutes or until cookies are set. *Do not overbake.* Cool 2 minutes on baking sheet. Remove cookies to foil to cool completely.

Makes about 3 dozen cookies

Original Nestlé® Toll House® Chocolate Chip Cookies

2¼ cups all-purpose flour
1 teaspoon baking soda
1 teaspoon salt
1 cup (2 sticks) butter or margarine, softened
¾ cup granulated sugar
¾ cup packed brown sugar
1 teaspoon vanilla extract
2 large eggs
2 cups (12-ounce package) NESTLÉ® TOLL HOUSE®
    Semi-Sweet Chocolate Morsels
1 cup chopped nuts

PREHEAT oven to 375°F.

COMBINE flour, baking soda and salt in small bowl. Beat butter, granulated sugar, brown sugar and vanilla in large mixer bowl until creamy. Add eggs, one at a time, beating well after each addition. Gradually beat in flour mixture. Stir in morsels and nuts. Drop by rounded tablespoons onto *ungreased* baking sheets.

BAKE for 9 to 11 minutes or until golden brown. Cool on baking sheets for 2 minutes; remove to wire racks to cool completely.

Makes about 5 dozen cookies

Pan Cookie Variation: **GREASE** 15×10-inch jelly-roll pan. Prepare dough as above. Spread into prepared pan. Bake for 20 to 25 minutes or until golden brown. Cool in pan on wire rack. Makes 4 dozen bars.

Slice and Bake Cookie Variation: **PREPARE** dough as above. Divide in half; wrap in wax paper. Refrigerate for 1 hour or until firm. Shape each half into 15-inch log; wrap in wax paper. Refrigerate for 30 minutes.* Preheat oven to 375°F. Cut into ½-inch-thick slices; place on *ungreased* baking sheets. Bake for 8 to 10 minutes or until golden brown. Cool on baking sheets for 2 minutes; remove to wire racks to cool completely. Makes about 5 dozen cookies.

May be stored in refrigerator for up to 1 week or in freezer for up to 8 weeks.

Crunchy Chocolate Chip Cookies

2¼ cups unsifted all-purpose flour
1 teaspoon ARM & HAMMER® Baking Soda
1 teaspoon salt
1 cup softened margarine or butter
¾ cup granulated sugar
¾ cup packed brown sugar
1 teaspoon vanilla extract
2 eggs
2 cups (12 ounces) semi-sweet chocolate chips
1 cup chopped nuts (peanuts, walnuts or pecans)

Preheat oven to 375°F. Sift together flour, Baking Soda and salt in small bowl. Beat margarine, sugars and vanilla in large bowl with electric mixer until creamy. Beat in eggs. Gradually add flour mixture; mix well. Stir in chocolate chips and nuts. Drop by rounded teaspoons onto *ungreased* cookie sheets. Bake 8 minutes or until lightly browned.

Makes about 8 dozen 2-inch cookies

Oatmeal Brownie Drops

½ cup (1 stick) butter or margarine, softened
¾ cup sugar
2 eggs
1 teaspoon vanilla extract
1 cup all-purpose flour
½ cup HERSHEY'S Cocoa
¼ teaspoon baking soda
1 cup quick-cooking oats
1 cup HERSHEY'S MINI CHIPS™ Semi-Sweet Chocolate
   Chips

1. Heat oven to 350°F.

2. Beat together butter and sugar in large bowl until creamy. Add eggs and vanilla; beat well. Stir together flour, cocoa and baking soda; gradually add to butter mixture, blending thoroughly. Stir in oats and small chocolate chips. Drop dough by tablespoonfuls onto *ungreased* cookie sheet.

3. Bake 7 to 8 minutes or until cookie begins to set. *Do not overbake.* Remove from cookie sheet to wire rack. Cool completely.

Makes about 3½ dozen cookies

Flowers may be nature's sweetest offering, but cookies run a close second.

Choc-Oat-Chip Cookies

1¾ cups all-purpose flour
1 teaspoon baking soda
½ teaspoon salt (optional)
1¼ cups packed brown sugar
1 cup (2 sticks) butter or margarine, softened
½ cup granulated sugar
2 large eggs
2 tablespoons milk
2 teaspoons vanilla extract
2½ cups quick or old fashioned oats
2 cups (12-ounce package) NESTLÉ® TOLL HOUSE®
   Semi-Sweet Chocolate Morsels
1 cup coarsely chopped nuts (optional)

PREHEAT oven to 375°F.

COMBINE flour, baking soda and salt in small bowl. Beat brown sugar, butter and granulated sugar in large mixer bowl until creamy. Beat in eggs, milk and vanilla extract. Gradually beat in flour mixture. Stir in oats, morsels and nuts; mix well. Drop by rounded tablespoons onto *ungreased* baking sheets.

BAKE for 9 to 10 minutes for a chewy cookie; 12 to 13 minutes for a crispy cookie. Cool on baking sheets for 1 minute; remove to wire racks to cool completely.   *Makes about 4 dozen cookies*

Oatmeal Scotchies

1 cup (2 sticks) margarine or butter, softened
¾ cup granulated sugar
¾ cup firmly packed brown sugar
2 eggs
1 teaspoon vanilla *or* 2 teaspoons grated orange peel (about 1 orange)
1¼ cups all-purpose flour
1 teaspoon baking soda
½ teaspoon salt (optional)
½ teaspoon ground cinnamon
3 cups QUAKER® Oats (quick or old fashioned, uncooked)
1 (12-ounce) package (2 cups) NESTLÉ® TOLL HOUSE® Butterscotch Flavored Morsels

Heat oven to 375°F. Beat together margarine, sugars, eggs and vanilla until creamy. Gradually add combined flour, baking soda, salt and cinnamon; mix well. Stir in remaining ingredients. Drop by level measuring tablespoonfuls onto *ungreased* cookie sheets. Bake 7 to 8 minutes for a chewy cookie or 9 to 10 minutes for a crisp cookie. Cool 2 minutes on cookie sheets; remove to wire rack. Cool completely.   *Makes about 4 dozen cookies*

Hershey's "Perfectly Chocolate" Chocolate Chip Cookies

2¼ cups all-purpose flour
⅓ cup HERSHEY'S Cocoa
1 teaspoon baking soda
½ teaspoon salt
1 cup (2 sticks) butter or margarine, softened
¾ cup granulated sugar
¾ cup packed light brown sugar
1 teaspoon vanilla extract
2 eggs
2 cups (12-ounce package) HERSHEY'S Semi-Sweet Chocolate Chips
1 cup chopped nuts (optional)

1. Heat oven to 375°F.

2. Stir together flour, cocoa, baking soda and salt. Beat butter, granulated sugar, brown sugar and vanilla in large bowl on medium speed of mixer until creamy. Add eggs; beat well. Gradually add flour mixture, beating until well blended. Stir in chocolate chips and nuts, if desired. Drop by rounded teaspoons onto *ungreased* cookie sheet.

3. Bake 8 to 10 minutes or until set. Cool slightly; remove from cookie sheet to wire rack. *Makes about 5 dozen cookies*

Chewy Cherry Chocolate Chip Cookies

½ **Butter Flavor CRISCO® Stick or ½ cup Butter Flavor CRISCO® all-vegetable shortening**
½ **cup granulated sugar**
½ **cup firmly packed brown sugar**
½ **cup dairy sour cream**
1 **egg**
1 **tablespoon maraschino cherry juice**
¾ **teaspoon vanilla**
1¼ **cups all-purpose flour**
½ **teaspoon baking soda**
¼ **teaspoon salt**
1 **cup semi-sweet chocolate chips**
½ **cup chopped pecans**
¼ **cup well-drained chopped maraschino cherries**

1. Heat oven to 375°F. Place sheets of foil on countertop for cooling cookies.

2. Combine shortening, granulated sugar and brown sugar in large bowl. Beat at medium speed of electric mixer until well blended. Beat in sour cream, egg, cherry juice and vanilla.

3. Combine flour, baking soda and salt. Mix into creamed mixture at low speed until well blended. Stir in chocolate chips, nuts and cherries.

4. Drop rounded tablespoonfuls of dough 2 inches apart onto *ungreased* baking sheet.

5. Bake at 375°F for 10 to 12 minutes or until set. *Do not overbake.* Cool 2 minutes on baking sheet. Remove cookies to foil to cool completely.

Makes about 3 dozen cookies

Peanut Butter Cocoa Cookies

1 **Butter Flavor CRISCO® Stick or 1 cup Butter Flavor CRISCO® all-vegetable shortening**
1 **cup granulated sugar**
1 **cup firmly packed brown sugar**
1 **cup JIF® Extra Crunchy Peanut Butter**
2 **eggs**
1 **teaspoon vanilla**
2 **cups all-purpose flour**
½ **cup unsweetened cocoa powder**
1 **teaspoon baking powder**
1 **teaspoon baking soda**
1 **cup milk chocolate chips**

1. Heat oven to 350°F. Place sheets of foil on countertop for cooling cookies.

2. Combine shortening, granulated sugar, brown sugar and peanut butter in large bowl. Beat at medium speed of electric mixer until well blended. Beat in eggs and vanilla. Beat until blended.

3. Combine flour, cocoa, baking powder and baking soda. Mix into creamed mixture at low speed until just blended. Stir in milk chocolate chips.

4. Drop rounded tablespoonfuls of dough 2 inches apart onto *ungreased* baking sheet.

5. Bake at 350°F for 10 to 12 minutes or until edges are lightly browned. *Do not overbake.* Cool 2 minutes on baking sheet. Remove cookies to foil to cool completely.   *Makes about 6 dozen cookies*

Chocolate Chip Almond Oatmeal Cookies

1 Butter Flavor CRISCO® Stick or 1 cup Butter Flavor
    CRISCO® all-vegetable shortening
1 cup granulated sugar
1 cup firmly packed dark brown sugar
2 large eggs
1 teaspoon vanilla
½ teaspoon almond extract
2 cups all-purpose flour
1 teaspoon baking soda
½ teaspoon salt
2 cups oats
9 ounces semi-sweet chocolate chips
1 cup slivered almonds

1. Heat oven to 350°F.

2. Combine shortening and sugars in large bowl. Beat at medium speed with electric mixer until well blended. Beat in eggs, vanilla and almond extract until well blended.

3. Combine flour, baking soda and salt in medium bowl. Add to creamed mixture; mix well. Add oats; mix well. Add chocolate chips and almonds.

4. Spray cookie sheets with CRISCO® No-Stick Cooking Spray. Drop dough by tablespoonfuls 2 inches apart onto prepared cookie sheets. Bake at 350°F for 10 to 12 minutes or until lightly browned. Cool on cookie sheets 4 minutes; transfer to cooling racks.

Makes about 4 dozen cookies

Chocolate Orange Dreams

Cookies
- **1 Butter Flavor CRISCO® Stick or 1 cup Butter Flavor CRISCO® all-vegetable shortening plus additional for greasing**
- **1 cup granulated sugar**
- **1 package (3 ounces) cream cheese, softened**
- **2 eggs**
- **2 teaspoons grated orange peel**
- **2 teaspoons strained fresh orange juice**
- **½ teaspoon salt**
- **2 cups all-purpose flour**
- **1 cup (6-ounce package) semi-sweet chocolate chips**

Glaze
- **½ cup confectioners' sugar**
- **2½ teaspoons strained fresh orange juice**
- **1½ teaspoons orange flavor liqueur**

1. Heat oven to 350°F. Grease baking sheet with shortening. Place sheets of foil on countertop for cooling cookies.

2. For cookies, combine shortening, granulated sugar and cream cheese in large bowl. Beat at medium speed of electric mixer until well blended. Beat in eggs, orange peel, 2 teaspoons orange juice and salt. Add flour gradually at low speed. Mix until well blended. Add chocolate chips. Drop by rounded teaspoonfuls 2 inches apart onto prepared baking sheet.

3. Bake at 350°F for 8 to 10 minutes or until light brown around edges. *Do not overbake.*

4. For glaze (prepare while cookies are baking), combine confectioners' sugar, 2½ teaspoons orange juice and liqueur. Stir until well blended. Brush on cookies immediately upon removing from oven. Cool 2 minutes on baking sheet. Remove cookies to foil to cool completely.

Makes about 4 dozen cookies

Butterscotch Sugar Drops

    1 cup (2 sticks) butter or margarine, softened
    1 cup sugar
    2 eggs
    ½ teaspoon vanilla extract
  2½ cups all-purpose flour
    1 teaspoon baking soda
    ½ teaspoon salt
  1⅔ cups (10-ounce package) HERSHEY.S Butterscotch Chips
  1¼ cups chopped dried apricots

1. Heat oven to 350°F.

2. Beat butter and sugar in large bowl until well blended. Add eggs and vanilla; beat well. Stir together flour, baking soda and salt; gradually add to butter mixture, beating until well blended. Stir in chips and apricots. Drop by teaspoons onto *ungreased* cookie sheets.

3. Bake 8 to 10 minutes or until lightly browned around edges. Cool slightly; remove from cookie sheet to wire rack. Cool completely.

Makes about 7 dozen cookies

Double Chocolate Cranberry Chunkies

1¾ cups all-purpose flour
⅓ cup unsweetened cocoa powder
½ teaspoon baking powder
½ teaspoon salt
1 cup (2 sticks) butter, softened
1 cup granulated sugar
½ cup packed brown sugar
1 egg
1 teaspoon vanilla
2 cups semisweet chocolate chunks or large chocolate chips
¾ cup dried cranberries or dried tart cherries
    Additional granulated sugar

1. Preheat oven to 350°F.

2. Combine flour, cocoa, baking powder and salt in small bowl; set aside. Beat butter, 1 cup granulated sugar and brown sugar in large bowl with electric mixer at medium speed until light and fluffy. Beat in egg and vanilla until well blended. Gradually beat in flour mixture on low speed until blended. Stir in chocolate chunks and cranberries.

3. Drop dough by level ¼ cupfuls onto *ungreased* cookie sheets, spacing 3 inches apart. Flatten dough until 2 inches in diameter with bottom of glass that has been dipped in additional granulated sugar.

4. Bake 11 to 12 minutes or until cookies are set. Cool cookies 2 minutes on cookie sheets; transfer to wire racks. Cool completely.

Makes about 1 dozen (4-inch) cookies

Chocolate Oatmeal Chippers

1¼ cups all-purpose flour
½ cup **NESTLÉ® TOLL HOUSE®** Baking Cocoa
1 teaspoon baking soda
¼ teaspoon salt
1 cup (2 sticks) butter or margarine, softened
1 cup packed brown sugar
½ cup granulated sugar
1 teaspoon vanilla extract
2 large eggs
1¾ cups (11½-ounce package) **NESTLÉ® TOLL HOUSE®** Milk
   Chocolate Morsels
1¾ cups quick or old-fashioned oats
1 cup chopped nuts (optional)

PREHEAT oven to 375°F.

COMBINE flour, cocoa, baking soda and salt in medium bowl. Beat butter, brown sugar, granulated sugar and vanilla in large mixer bowl until creamy. Beat in eggs. Gradually beat in flour mixture. Stir in morsels, oats and nuts, if desired. Drop dough by rounded tablespoons onto *ungreased* baking sheets.

BAKE for 9 to 12 minutes or until edges are set but centers are still soft. Cool on baking sheets for 2 minutes; remove to wire racks to cool completely.   *Makes about 4 dozen cookies*

Bar Cookie Variation: **PREHEAT** oven to 350°F. Grease 15×10-inch jelly-roll pan. Prepare dough as above. Spread into prepared pan. Bake for 25 to 30 minutes. Cool in pan on wire rack. Makes about 4 dozen bars.

Peanut Butter Oatmeal Treats

1¾ cups all-purpose flour
1 teaspoon baking soda
½ teaspoon salt
½ cup butter or margarine, softened
½ cup SMUCKER'S® Creamy Natural Peanut Butter or
   LAURA SCUDDER'S® Smooth Old-Fashioned Peanut
   Butter
1 cup granulated sugar
1 cup firmly-packed light brown sugar
2 eggs
¼ cup milk
1 teaspoon vanilla
2½ cups uncooked oats
1 cup semi-sweet chocolate chips

Combine flour, baking soda and salt; set aside. In large mixing bowl, combine butter, peanut butter, sugar and brown sugar. Beat until light and creamy. Beat in eggs, milk and vanilla. Stir in flour mixture, oats and chocolate chips. Drop dough by rounded teaspoonfuls about 3 inches apart onto *ungreased* cookie sheets.

Bake at 350°F for 15 minutes or until lightly browned.

Makes 3½ dozen cookies

Hershey's Chocolate Chip Blondies

6 tablespoons butter or margarine, softened
¾ cup packed light brown sugar
1 egg
1 tablespoon milk
1 teaspoon vanilla extract
1 cup all-purpose flour
½ teaspoon baking soda
⅛ teaspoon salt
2 cups (12-ounce package) HERSHEY'S Semi-Sweet
    Chocolate Chips
½ cup coarsely chopped nuts (optional)

1. Heat oven to 350°F. Grease 9-inch square baking pan.

2. Beat butter and brown sugar in large bowl until fluffy. Add egg, milk and vanilla; beat well. Stir together flour, baking soda and salt; add to butter mixture. Stir in chocolate chips and nuts, if desired; spread in prepared pan.

3. Bake 20 to 25 minutes or until lightly browned. Cool completely; cut into bars. *Makes about 1½ dozen bars*

Heavenly Almond Treats

1 Butter Flavor CRISCO® Stick or 1 cup Butter Flavor CRISCO® all-vegetable shortening
²/₃ **cup firmly packed dark brown sugar**
½ **cup granulated sugar**
1 egg, lightly beaten
¼ **cup sweetened condensed milk**
1 teaspoon almond extract
1 teaspoon vanilla
2 cups all-purpose flour
1 teaspoon baking soda
1 teaspoon salt
2 cups flaked coconut
2 cups milk chocolate chips
1 cup slivered almonds

1. Heat oven to 375°F. Place sheets of foil on countertop for cooling cookies.

2. Combine shortening, brown sugar and granulated sugar in large bowl. Beat at medium speed of electric mixer until well blended.

3. Combine egg, milk, almond extract and vanilla. Mix into creamed mixture at low speed until blended.

4. Combine flour, baking soda and salt. Mix into creamed mixture at low speed until just blended. Stir in, one at a time, coconut, chocolate chips and almonds.

5. Drop rounded tablespoonfuls of dough 2 inches apart onto *ungreased* baking sheet. Shape dough into 3×1-inch ovals.

6. Bake at 375°F for 12 minutes, or until golden brown. *Do not overbake.* Cool 2 minutes on baking sheet. Remove cookies to foil to cool completely.   *Makes about 4 dozen cookies*

Sour Cream Chocolate Chip Cookies

  1 Butter Flavor CRISCO® Stick or 1 cup Butter Flavor
      CRISCO® all-vegetable shortening plus additional
      for greasing
  1 cup firmly packed brown sugar
  ½ cup granulated sugar
  1 egg
  ½ cup dairy sour cream
  ¼ cup warm honey
  2 teaspoons vanilla
  2½ cups all-purpose flour
  1½ teaspoons baking powder
  ½ teaspoon salt
  2 cups semi-sweet or milk chocolate chips
  1 cup coarsely chopped walnuts

1. Heat oven to 375°F. Grease cookie sheets. Place sheets of foil on countertop for cooling cookies.

2. Combine shortening, brown sugar and granulated sugar in large bowl. Beat at medium speed of electric mixer until well blended. Beat in egg, sour cream, honey and vanilla. Beat until just blended.

3. Combine flour, baking powder and salt. Mix into creamed mixture at low speed until just blended. Stir in chocolate chips and nuts.

4. Drop slightly rounded measuring tablespoonfuls of dough 2 inches apart onto prepared sheet.

5. Bake at 375°F 10 to 12 minutes or until set. *Do not overbake.* Cool 2 minutes on baking sheet. Remove to foil to cool completely.

Makes about 5 dozen cookies

Fruit and Nut Chippers

        1 cup (2 sticks) butter, softened
      ¾ cup granulated sugar
      ¾ cup packed light brown sugar
        2 large eggs
        1 teaspoon vanilla
    2¼ cups all-purpose flour
        1 teaspoon baking soda
      ½ teaspoon salt
        1 package (11½ ounces) milk chocolate chips
        1 cup chopped dried apricots
        1 cup chopped pecans or walnuts

1. Preheat oven to 375°F. Beat butter, granulated sugar and brown sugar in large bowl until light and fluffy. Beat in eggs and vanilla. Add combined flour, baking soda and salt. Beat until well blended. Stir in chips, apricots and pecans.

2. Drop dough by heaping teaspoonfuls 2 inches apart onto *ungreased* cookie sheets.

3. Bake 9 to 10 minutes or until edges are golden brown. Let cookies stand on cookie sheets 2 minutes. Remove cookies to wire racks; cool completely.   *Makes about 5 dozen cookies*

Mom and Katie's Crunchy Chocolate Chip Cookies

  1 Butter Flavor CRISCO® Stick or 1 cup Butter Flavor
      CRISCO® all-vegetable shortening
 ¾ cup firmly packed dark brown sugar
 ½ cup granulated sugar
  1 egg, lightly beaten
  1 teaspoon vanilla
1½ cups all-purpose flour
  1 teaspoon baking soda
 ½ teaspoon salt
 ½ teaspoon ground nutmeg
1½ cups semisweet chocolate chips
  1 cup uncooked oats
  1 cup finely chopped pecans
 ½ cup honey crunch wheat germ

1. Heat oven to 375°F. Place sheets of foil on countertop for cooling cookies.

2. Combine shortening and sugars in large bowl. Beat until well blended. Mix in egg and vanilla.

3. Combine flour, baking soda, salt and nutmeg. Add to creamed mixture. Stir until well blended.

4. Combine chocolate chips, oats, pecans and wheat germ. Stir into dough. Mix well. Shape dough into 2-inch balls. Place 3 inches apart on *ungreased* baking sheet. Flatten with hand to about ⅜-inch thickness.

5. Bake for 7 to 8 minutes or until golden brown. *Do not overbake.* Cool 2 minutes on baking sheet. Remove cookies to foil to cool completely.   *Makes 2 to 2½ dozen cookies*

Cocoa-Chip Cookies

⅔ cup shortening
1½ cups sugar
2 eggs
⅔ cup dairy sour cream
1 teaspoon vanilla extract
2 cups all-purpose flour
½ cup HERSHEY'S Cocoa or HERSHEY'S Dutch Processed
    Cocoa
½ teaspoon baking soda
½ teaspoon salt
2 cups (12-ounce package) HERSHEY'S MINI CHIPS™
    Semi-Sweet Chocolate Chips

1. Heat oven to 375°F. Lightly grease cookie sheet.

2. Beat shortening and sugar in large bowl until blended. Add eggs, sour cream and vanilla; beat well. Stir together flour, cocoa, baking soda and salt; gradually add to shortening mixture, beating until well blended. Stir in small chocolate chips. Drop by teaspoons onto prepared cookie sheet.

3. Bake 8 to 10 minutes or until puffed and slightly cracked. Remove from cookie sheet to wire rack. Cool completely.

Makes about 5½ dozen cookies

Double Chocolate Cherry Cookies

Prep Time: 25 minutes
Bake Time: 8 to 10 minutes

1¼ cups (2½ sticks) butter or margarine, softened
1¾ cups sugar
2 eggs
1 tablespoon vanilla extract
3½ cups all-purpose flour
¾ cup unsweetened cocoa
½ teaspoon baking powder
½ teaspoon baking soda
¼ teaspoon salt
2 (6-ounce) jars maraschino cherries, well drained and halved (about 60 cherries)
1 (6-ounce) package semi-sweet chocolate chips
1 (14-ounce) can EAGLE® BRAND Sweetened Condensed Milk (NOT evaporated milk)

1. Preheat oven to 350°F. In large mixing bowl, beat butter and sugar until fluffy. Add eggs and vanilla; mix well.

2. In large mixing bowl, combine dry ingredients; stir into butter mixture (dough will be stiff). Shape into 1-inch balls. Place 1 inch apart on *ungreased* baking sheets.

3. Press cherry half into center of each cookie. Bake 8 to 10 minutes. Cool.

4. In heavy saucepan over medium heat, melt chips with Eagle Brand; cook until mixture thickens, about 3 minutes. Frost each cookie, covering cherry. Store loosely covered at room temperature.

Makes about 10 dozen cookies

Double Chocolate Pecan Cookies: Prepare and shape dough as directed above, omitting cherries. Flatten. Bake and frost as directed. Garnish each cookie with pecan half.

Honey Chocolate Chippers

1 cup honey
1 cup butter or margarine, softened
1 egg yolk
1 teaspoon vanilla extract
2 cups all-purpose flour
1 cup oats
½ teaspoon baking soda
½ teaspoon salt
1 cup chopped toasted pecans
1 cup (6 ounces) semi-sweet chocolate chips

In medium bowl, beat honey and butter until creamy but not fluffy. Beat in egg yolk and vanilla. In separate bowl, combine flour, oats, baking soda and salt. Stir dry ingredients into wet mixture until thoroughly blended. Mix in pecans and chocolate chips. Chill dough for 30 minutes. Drop dough by rounded tablespoons onto *ungreased* cookie sheets. Flatten each cookie with a spoon. Bake at 350°F for 15 to 20 minutes, or until tops are dry. Cool on wire racks.

Makes 2 dozen

Favorite recipe from **National Honey Board**

Chocolatey and Nutty
Peanut Butter Cookies

1 Butter Flavor CRISCO® Stick or 1 cup Butter Flavor
CRISCO® all-vegetable shortening

¾ cup JIF® Extra Crunchy Peanut Butter

¾ cup granulated sugar

¾ cup firmly packed brown sugar

1 teaspoon vanilla

2 eggs

2¼ cups all-purpose flour

1 teaspoon baking soda

1 teaspoon salt

1 teaspoon cinnamon

2 cups semi-sweet chocolate chips

1 cup quick oats (not instant or old fashioned)

1. Heat oven to 375°F. Place sheets of foil on countertop for cooling cookies.

2. Combine shortening, peanut butter, granulated sugar, brown sugar and vanilla in large bowl. Beat at medium speed of electric mixer until well blended. Beat in eggs.

3. Combine flour, baking soda, salt and cinnamon. Mix into creamed mixture at low speed until blended. Stir in chocolate chips and oats with spoon.

4. Drop rounded tablespoonfuls of dough 2 inches apart onto *ungreased* baking sheet.

5. Bake at 375°F for 7 to 9 minutes or until cookies are golden on bottom. *Do not overbake.* Cool 2 minutes on baking sheet. Remove cookies to foil to cool completely.   *Makes about 4½ dozen cookies*

Molasses Snaps

2¼ cups all-purpose flour
2 teaspoons baking soda
1 cup packed light brown sugar
¾ cup (1½ sticks) butter or margarine, softened
1 egg
¼ cup light molasses
1⅔ cups (10-ounce package) REESE'S® Peanut Butter Chips
Granulated sugar

1. Stir together flour and baking soda. Beat brown sugar and butter in large bowl; add egg and molasses, beating until smooth. Stir in flour mixture and peanut butter chips until well blended. Cover; refrigerate 1 hour.

2. Heat oven to 350°F. Grease and flour cookie sheet.

3. Shape dough into 1-inch balls; roll in granulated sugar. Place on prepared cookie sheet.

4. Bake 8 to 10 minutes or until tops begin cracking; immediately remove from cookie sheet to wire rack. Cool completely.

Makes about 5 dozen cookies

Double Chocolate Banana Cookies

Prep Time: 15 minutes
Chill Time: 1 hour
Bake Time: 17 minutes per batch

   3 to 4 extra-ripe medium DOLE® Bananas
   2 cups oats
   2 cups sugar
1¾ cups all-purpose flour
  ½ cup unsweetened cocoa powder
  1 teaspoon baking soda
  ½ teaspoon salt
1¼ cups margarine, melted
  2 eggs, slightly beaten
  2 cups semisweet chocolate chips
  1 cup chopped natural almonds, toasted

• Purée bananas in blender; measure 2 cups for recipe.

• Combine oats, sugar, flour, cocoa, baking soda and salt until well mixed. Stir in bananas, margarine and eggs until blended. Stir in chocolate chips and almonds.

• Refrigerate batter 1 hour or until mixture becomes partially firm (batter runs during baking if too soft).

• Preheat oven to 350°F. Measure ¼-cup batter for each cookie; drop onto greased cookie sheet. Flatten slightly with spatula.

• Bake 15 to 17 minutes until cookies are golden brown. Remove to wire rack to cool. *Makes about 2½ dozen (3-inch) cookies*

Keepsake Bars

Luscious Lemon Bars

- 2 **cups all-purpose flour**
- 1 **cup (2 sticks) butter**
- ½ **cup powdered sugar**
- 4 **teaspoons grated lemon peel, divided**
- ¼ **teaspoon salt**
- 1 **cup granulated sugar**
- 3 **large eggs**
- ⅓ **cup fresh lemon juice**
  Sifted powdered sugar

1. Preheat oven to 350°F. Grease 13×9-inch baking pan; set aside. Place flour, butter, powdered sugar, 1 teaspoon lemon peel and salt in food processor. Process until mixture forms coarse crumbs.

2. Press mixture evenly into prepared baking pan. Bake 18 to 20 minutes or until golden brown.

3. Beat granulated sugar, eggs, lemon juice and remaining 3 teaspoons lemon peel in medium bowl with electric mixer at medium speed until well blended.

4. Pour mixture evenly over warm crust. Return to oven; bake 18 to 20 minutes or until center is set and edges are golden brown. Remove pan to wire rack; cool completely.

5. Dust with sifted powdered sugar; cut into bars. Store tightly covered at room temperature. *Do not freeze.*

Makes 3 dozen bars

Butterscotch Blondies

¾ **cup (1½ sticks) butter or margarine, softened**
¾ **cup packed light brown sugar**
½ **cup granulated sugar**
2 **eggs**
2 **cups all-purpose flour**
1 **teaspoon baking soda**
½ **teaspoon salt**
1⅔ **cups (10-ounce package) HERSHEY'S Butterscotch Chips**
1 **cup chopped nuts (optional)**

1. Heat oven to 350°F. Grease 13×9×2-inch baking pan.

2. Beat butter, brown sugar and granulated sugar in large bowl until creamy. Add eggs; beat well. Stir together flour, baking soda and salt; gradually add to butter mixture, blending well. Stir in butterscotch chips and nuts, if desired. Spread into prepared pan.

3. Bake 30 to 35 minutes or until top is golden brown and center is set. Cool completely in pan on wire rack. Cut into bars.

Makes about 36 bars

Absolutely Wonderful Pecan Bars

1½ **cups quick or old-fashioned oats**
1½ **cups all-purpose flour**
  2 **cups DOMINO® Dark Brown Sugar, packed, divided**
1½ **cups butter (not margarine), divided**
1½ **cups or 1 (7-ounce) package pecan halves**
  1 **cup DOMINO® Granulated Sugar**
⅓ **cup heavy cream**
  2 **teaspoons vanilla**

In large bowl, combine oats, flour and 1 cup brown sugar. Cut ½ cup butter into mixture until coarse and crumbly. Press into 13×9-inch baking pan. Place pecans evenly over crumb mixture.

In heavy saucepan, combine remaining 1 cup brown sugar, granulated sugar and 1 cup butter. Bring to a rolling boil over medium heat, stirring constantly. Boil 3 minutes; remove from heat. Stir in cream and vanilla until well blended; pour over pecans. Bake in preheated 350°F oven 35 to 40 minutes. Cool in pan; cut into bars.

Makes 48 bars

Chewy Red Raspberry Bars

1 cup firmly packed light brown sugar
½ cup butter or margarine, room temperature
½ teaspoon almond extract
1 cup all-purpose flour
1 cup quick-cooking or old-fashioned oats
1 teaspoon baking powder
½ cup SMUCKER'S® Red Raspberry Preserves

Combine brown sugar and butter; beat until fluffy. Beat in almond extract. Mix in flour, oats and baking powder until crumbly. Reserve ¼ cup mixture; pat remaining mixture into bottom of greased 8-inch square baking pan. Dot preserves over crumb mixture in pan; sprinkle with reserved crumb mixture.

Bake at 350°F for 30 to 40 minutes or until brown. Cool on wire rack. Cut into bars. *Makes 12 bars*

"Blondie" Brownies

½ **Butter Flavor CRISCO® Stick or ½ cup Butter Flavor CRISCO® all-vegetable shortening plus additional for greasing**
1 **tablespoon milk**
1 **cup firmly packed brown sugar**
1 **egg**
1 **cup all-purpose flour**
½ **teaspoon baking powder**
⅛ **teaspoon salt**
1 **teaspoon vanilla**
½ **cup chopped walnuts**

1. Heat oven to 350°F. Grease 8×8×2-inch pan with shortening. Place cooling rack on countertop.

2. Combine shortening and milk in large microwave-safe bowl. Microwave at MEDIUM (50% power). Stir after 1 minute. Repeat until melted (or melt on rangetop in large saucepan on low heat). Stir in sugar. Stir in egg quickly. Combine flour, baking powder and salt. Stir into sugar mixture. Stir in vanilla and nuts. Spread in prepared pan.

3. Bake at 350°F for 27 to 30 minutes or until toothpick inserted into center comes out clean. *Do not overbake.* Cool in pan on cooling rack. Cut into 2×2-inch squares. *Makes 16 squares*

Cranberry Almond Squares

    3 cups cranberries
    1 cup raisins
    1 cup chopped peeled apple
    1 cup unsweetened apple juice
    1 tablespoon granulated sugar
 1½ cups whole wheat flour
    1 cup regular oats, uncooked
    ⅓ cup firmly packed brown sugar
    1 teaspoon ground cinnamon
    ⅛ teaspoon salt
    ½ cup molasses
    ¼ cup CRISCO® Oil*
    2 tablespoons slivered almonds, toasted, chopped

*Use your favorite Crisco Oil product.

1. Heat oven to 350°F. Place cooling rack on countertop. Lightly oil 13×9-inch pan. Combine cranberries, raisins, apple, apple juice and granulated sugar in saucepan. Bring to a boil. Cook 5 minutes or until cranberry skins pop, stirring occasionally. Reduce heat and simmer, uncovered, 10 minutes. Stir occasionally. Cool.

2. Combine flour, oats, brown sugar, cinnamon and salt in medium bowl. Combine molasses and oil; add to flour mixture. Toss with fork until mixture resembles coarse meal.

3. Press 2 cups flour mixture in bottom of prepared pan. Top with cranberry mixture. Spread evenly. Combine remaining flour mixture and almonds. Sprinkle over cranberry mixture. Press lightly.

4. Bake at 350°F for 35 minutes or until golden. *Do not overbake.* Remove to cooling rack to cool completely. Cut into squares. Store loosely covered. *Makes 24 squares*

Chocolate Coconut Pecan Squares

¾ cup margarine or butter, divided
¾ cup sugar, divided
1¼ cups all-purpose flour
2 tablespoons heavy cream
1¾ cups PLANTERS® Pecans, coarsely chopped
1 cup flaked coconut
4 ounces semisweet chocolate, coarsely chopped

1. Beat ½ cup margarine and ¼ cup sugar in bowl with mixer until creamy. Blend in flour until dough forms. Press on bottom of *ungreased* 9×9×2-inch baking pan. Bake at 350°F for 18 to 20 minutes or until edges are lightly browned.

2. Heat remaining ½ cup sugar, ¼ cup margarine and heavy cream in saucepan, stirring until margarine melts and mixture is blended. Stir in pecans; set aside.

3. Sprinkle coconut and chocolate evenly over crust. Top with pecan mixture, spreading evenly. Bake for 20 to 25 minutes more or until golden. Cool completely; cut into squares. *Makes 16 squares*

Fruit and Nut Bars

  1 **cup unsifted all-purpose flour**
  1 **cup quick oats**
 ⅔ **cup brown sugar**
  2 **teaspoons baking soda**
 ½ **teaspoon salt**
 ½ **teaspoon cinnamon**
 ⅔ **cup buttermilk**
  3 **tablespoons vegetable oil**
  2 **egg whites, lightly beaten**
  1 **Washington Golden Delicious apple, cored and chopped**
 ½ **cup dried cranberries or raisins, chopped**
 ¼ **cup chopped nuts**
  2 **tablespoons flaked coconut (optional)**

1. Heat oven to 375°F. Lightly grease 9-inch square baking pan. In large mixing bowl, combine flour, oats, brown sugar, baking soda, salt and cinnamon; stir to blend.

2. Add buttermilk, oil and egg whites; beat with electric mixer just until mixed. Stir in apple, dried fruit and nuts; spread evenly in pan and top with coconut, if desired. Bake 20 to 25 minutes or until cake tester inserted in center comes out clean. Cool and cut into 10 bars.

Makes 10 bars

Favorite recipe from **Washington Apple Commission**

Almond Toffee Bars

¾ **cup butter or margarine, softened**
¾ **cup packed brown sugar**
1½ **cups all-purpose flour**
½ **teaspoon almond extract**
½ **teaspoon vanilla extract**
¼ **teaspoon salt**
 1 **package (6 ounces) semi-sweet real chocolate pieces**
¾ **cup BLUE DIAMOND® Chopped Natural Almonds,**
    toasted

Preheat oven to 350°F. Cream butter and sugar; blend in flour.
Add extracts and salt, mixing well. Spread in bottom of *ungreased*
13×9×2-inch baking pan. Bake in 350°F oven for 15 to 20 minutes or
until deep golden brown. Remove from oven and sprinkle with
chocolate pieces. When chocolate has melted, spread evenly; sprinkle
with almonds. Cut into bars; cool.   *Makes about 40 bars*

Chunky Pecan Pie Bars

Crust
- 1½ cups all-purpose flour
- ½ cup (1 stick) butter or margarine, softened
- ¼ cup packed brown sugar

Filling
- 3 large eggs
- ¾ cup granulated sugar
- ¾ cup corn syrup
- 2 tablespoons butter or margarine, melted
- 1 teaspoon vanilla extract
- 1¾ cups (11.5-ounce package) NESTLÉ® TOLL HOUSE® Semi-Sweet Chocolate Chunks
- 1½ cups coarsely chopped pecans

PREHEAT oven to 350°F. Grease 13×9-inch baking pan.

For Crust
BEAT flour, butter and brown sugar in small mixer bowl until crumbly. Press into prepared baking pan.

BAKE for 12 to 15 minutes or until lightly browned.

For Filling
BEAT eggs, granulated sugar, corn syrup, butter and vanilla in medium bowl with wire whisk. Stir in chunks and nuts. Pour evenly over baked crust.

BAKE for 25 to 30 minutes or until set. Cool completely in pan on wire rack. Cut into bars. *Makes about 3 dozen bars*

Luscious Fresh Lemon Bars

Crust
- ½ **cup butter or margarine, softened**
- ½ **cup granulated sugar**
- **Grated peel of ½ SUNKIST® lemon**
- 1¼ **cups all-purpose flour**

Lemon Layer
- 4 **eggs**
- 1⅔ **cups granulated sugar**
- 3 **tablespoons all-purpose flour**
- ½ **teaspoon baking powder**
- **Grated peel of ½ SUNKIST® lemon**
- **Juice of 2 SUNKIST® lemons (6 tablespoons)**
- 1 **teaspoon vanilla extract**
- **Confectioners' sugar**

To make crust, in bowl blend together butter, granulated sugar and lemon peel. Gradually stir in flour to form a soft crumbly dough. Press evenly into bottom of foil-lined 13×9×2-inch baking pan. Bake at 350°F for 15 minutes.

Meanwhile, to prepare lemon layer, in large bowl whisk or beat eggs well. Stir together granulated sugar, flour and baking powder. Gradually whisk sugar mixture into beaten eggs. Stir or whisk in lemon peel, lemon juice and vanilla. Pour over hot baked crust. Return to oven and bake for 20 to 25 minutes or until top and sides are lightly browned. Cool. Using foil on two sides, lift out the cookie base and gently loosen foil along all sides. With a long wet knife, cut into bars or squares. Sprinkle tops with confectioners' sugar.

Makes about 3 dozen bars

Cinnamony Apple Streusel Bars

1¼ **cups graham cracker crumbs**
1¼ **cups all-purpose flour**
¾ **cup packed brown sugar, divided**
¼ **cup granulated sugar**
1 **teaspoon ground cinnamon**
¾ **cup butter, melted**
2 **cups chopped apples (2 medium apples, cored and peeled)**
Glaze (recipe follows)

Preheat oven to 350°F. Grease 13×9-inch baking pan. Combine graham cracker crumbs, flour, ½ cup brown sugar, granulated sugar, cinnamon and melted butter in large bowl until well blended; reserve 1 cup. Press remaining crumb mixture into bottom of prepared pan. Bake 8 minutes. Remove from oven; set aside.

Toss remaining ¼ cup brown sugar with apples in medium bowl until dissolved; arrange apples over baked crust. Sprinkle reserved 1 cup crumb mixture over filling. Bake 30 to 35 minutes or until apples are tender. Remove pan to wire rack; cool completely. Drizzle with Glaze. Cut into bars.   *Makes 3 dozen bars*

Glaze: Combine ½ cup powdered sugar and 1 tablespoon milk in small bowl until well blended.

Fabulous Fruit Bars

1½ cups all-purpose flour, divided
1½ cups sugar, divided
½ cup MOTT'S® Apple Sauce, divided
½ teaspoon baking powder
2 tablespoons margarine
½ cup chopped peeled apple
½ cup chopped dried apricots
½ cup chopped cranberries
1 whole egg
1 egg white
1 teaspoon lemon juice
½ teaspoon vanilla extract
1 teaspoon ground cinnamon

1. Preheat oven to 350°F. Spray 13×9-inch baking pan with nonstick cooking spray.

2. In medium bowl, combine 1¼ cups flour, ½ cup sugar, ⅓ cup apple sauce and baking powder. Cut in margarine with pastry blender or fork until mixture resembles coarse crumbs.

3. In large bowl, combine apple, apricots, cranberries, remaining apple sauce, whole egg, egg white, lemon juice and vanilla.

4. In small bowl, combine remaining 1 cup sugar, ¼ cup flour and cinnamon. Add to fruit mixture, stirring just until mixed.

5. Press half of crumb mixture evenly into bottom of prepared pan. Top with fruit mixture. Sprinkle with remaining crumb mixture.

6. Bake 40 minutes or until lightly browned. Broil, 4 inches from heat, 1 to 2 minutes or until golden brown. Cool on wire rack 15 minutes; cut into 16 bars. *Makes 16 servings*

Walnut Apple Dumpling Bars

6 tablespoons (¾ stick) butter or margarine
1 cup packed light brown sugar
1 cup all-purpose flour
1 teaspoon baking powder
1½ teaspoons ground cinnamon
2 eggs
1½ cups coarsely chopped California walnuts
1 Granny Smith or pippin apple, coarsely grated* (about
   1 cup lightly packed)
Powdered sugar

*It's not necessary to peel or core apple. Use hand-held grater, turning apple as you go, until only core remains.

Preheat oven to 350°F.

Melt butter in 3-quart saucepan. Add sugar. Stir until sugar is melted and mixture begins to bubble; cool. In small bowl combine flour, baking powder and cinnamon; mix to blend thoroughly. Beat eggs into butter mixture in saucepan, 1 at a time, then add flour mixture. Add walnuts and apple. Turn into buttered and floured 9-inch square baking pan; smooth top. Bake 25 to 35 minutes until toothpick inserted into center comes out clean and edges begin to pull away from sides of pan. Cool completely on rack. Cut into 3×1-inch bars. Garnish with powdered sugar. *Makes 24 bars*

Favorite recipe from **Walnut Marketing Board**

Holiday Red Raspberry Chocolate Bars

2½ cups all-purpose flour
  1 cup sugar
  ¾ cup finely chopped pecans
  1 cup (2 sticks) cold butter or margarine
  1 egg, beaten
  1 jar (12 ounces) seedless red raspberry jam
1⅔ cups HERSHEY'S Milk Chocolate Chips, HERSHEY'S
      Semi-Sweet Chocolate Chips, HERSHEY'S Raspberry
      Chips, or HERSHEY'S MINI KISSES™ Milk Chocolates

1. Heat oven to 350°F. Grease 13×9×2-inch baking pan.

2. Stir together flour, sugar, pecans, butter and egg in large bowl. Cut in butter with pastry blender or fork until mixture resembles coarse crumbs; set aside 1½ cups crumb mixture. Press remaining crumb mixture on bottom of prepared pan; spread jam over top. Sprinkle with chocolate chips. Sprinkle remaining crumb mixture evenly over top.

3. Bake 40 to 45 minutes or until lightly browned. Cool completely in pan on wire rack; cut into bars. *Makes 36 bars*

Gingerbread Apple Bars

  1 cup applesauce
  ½ cup raisins
  ⅓ cup unsulfured light molasses
  1 teaspoon baking soda
  2 eggs
  ¼ cup sugar
  ¼ cup CRISCO® Oil*
1½ cups all-purpose flour
  1 teaspoon ground cinnamon
  ½ teaspoon ground ginger
  ¼ teaspoon ground cloves
  ⅛ teaspoon salt

Use your favorite Crisco Oil product.

1. Heat oven to 350°F. Oil 8-inch square pan lightly.

2. Place applesauce and raisins in small saucepan. Cook and stir on low heat until mixture comes to a boil. Remove from heat. Stir in molasses and baking soda. Cool slightly.

3. Combine eggs and sugar in large bowl. Beat in ¼ cup oil gradually.

4. Combine flour, cinnamon, ginger, cloves and salt in small bowl. Add to egg mixture alternately with applesauce mixture, beginning and ending with flour mixture. Spoon into pan.

5. Bake at 350°F for 30 minutes or until toothpick inserted into center comes out clean. Cool in pan on cooling rack. Cut into bars. Serve warm or at room temperature. *Makes 1 dozen bars*

Layered Chocolate Cheese Bars

Prep Time: 15 minutes

- 1½ **cups graham cracker crumbs**
- ¾ **cup sugar, divided**
- ¼ **cup (½ stick) butter or margarine, melted**
- 1 **package (4 ounces) BAKER'S® GERMAN'S® Sweet Chocolate**
- 1 **package (8 ounces) PHILADELPHIA® Cream Cheese, softened**
- 1 **egg**
- 1 **cup BAKER'S® ANGEL FLAKE® Coconut**
- 1 **cup chopped nuts**

HEAT oven to 350°F.

MIX crumbs and ¼ cup of the sugar. Add butter; mix well. Press evenly onto bottom of 13×9-inch baking pan. Bake 10 minutes.

MEANWHILE microwave chocolate in microwaveable bowl on HIGH 1½ to 2 minutes or until almost melted, stirring halfway through heating time. Stir until chocolate is completely melted.

ADD cream cheese, egg and remaining ½ cup sugar; mix well. Spread evenly over baked crust. Top with coconut and nuts, pressing into cheese mixture.

BAKE for 30 minutes. Cool; cut into bars.   *Makes about 24 bars*

Orange Pumpkin Bars

Bars
- 1½ cups all-purpose flour
- 1 teaspoon baking powder
- 1 teaspoon pumpkin pie spice
- ½ teaspoon baking soda
- ½ teaspoon salt
- 1 cup solid pack canned pumpkin (not pumpkin pie filling)
- ¾ cup granulated sugar
- ⅔ cup CRISCO® Oil*
- 2 eggs
- ¼ cup firmly packed light brown sugar
- 2 tablespoons orange juice
- ½ cup chopped nuts
- ½ cup raisins

Icing
- 1½ cups confectioners' sugar
- 2 tablespoons orange juice
- 2 tablespoons butter or margarine, softened
- ½ teaspoon grated orange peel

Use your favorite Crisco Oil product.

1. Heat oven to 350°F. Grease and flour 12×8-inch baking dish; set aside. Place wire rack on countertop for cooling bars.

2. For bars, combine flour, baking powder, pumpkin pie spice, baking soda and salt in medium mixing bowl; set aside.

3. Combine pumpkin, granulated sugar, oil, eggs, brown sugar and orange juice in large mixing bowl. Beat at low speed of electric mixer until blended, scraping bowl constantly. Add flour mixture. Beat at medium speed until smooth, scraping bowl frequently. Stir in nuts and raisins. Pour into prepared pan. Bake at 350°F for 35 minutes or until center springs back when touched lightly. *Do not overbake.* Cool bars in pan on cooling rack.

4. For icing, combine all ingredients. Beat at medium speed of electric mixer until smooth. Spread over cooled base. Cut into bars.

Makes about 24 bars

Mott's® Chewy Oatmeal Raisin Squares

- **1 cup raisins**
- **1 cup rolled oats**
- **¾ cup boiling water**
- **1 cup granulated sugar**
- **½ cup MOTT'S® Natural Apple Sauce**
- **¼ cup MOTT'S® Grandma's® Molasses**
- **1 whole egg**
- **2 egg whites, lightly beaten**
- **2 tablespoons vegetable oil**
- **1 teaspoon vanilla extract**
- **2 cups all-purpose flour**
- **1½ teaspoons baking powder**
- **½ teaspoon baking soda**
- **1 teaspoon cinnamon**
- **½ teaspoon ground cloves**
- **½ teaspoon salt**

1. Preheat oven to 400°F. Spray 13×9-inch baking pan with nonstick cooking spray.

2. In medium bowl, combine raisins and rolled oats. Pour boiling water over ingredients; mix until moistened. Set aside.

3. In large bowl, combine sugar, apple sauce, molasses, whole egg, egg whites, oil and vanilla.

4. In separate medium bowl, combine flour, baking powder, baking soda, spices and salt.

5. Add flour mixture to apple sauce mixture; mix until ingredients are combined. Stir in raisin-oatmeal mixture.

6. Spread batter evenly into prepared pan. Bake 12 to 15 minutes. Place pan on cooling rack to cool.

7. Let cool 15 minutes before cutting into squares.

Makes 16 squares

Chewy Butterscotch Brownies

2½ cups all-purpose flour
2 teaspoons baking powder
½ teaspoon salt
1 cup (2 sticks) butter or margarine, softened
1¾ cups packed brown sugar
1 tablespoons vanilla extract
2 large eggs
1⅔ cups (11-ounce package) NESTLÉ® TOLL HOUSE®
   Butterscotch Flavored Morsels, *divided*
1 cup chopped nuts

PREHEAT oven to 350°F.

COMBINE flour, baking powder and salt in medium bowl. Beat butter, sugar and vanilla extract in large mixer bowl until creamy. Beat in eggs. Gradually beat in flour mixture. Stir in *1 cup* morsels and nuts. Spread into *ungreased* 13×9-inch baking pan. Sprinkle with *remaining* morsels.

BAKE for 30 to 40 minutes or until wooden pick inserted into center comes out clean. Cool in pan on wire rack.

Makes about 4 dozen brownies

Peachy Oatmeal Bars

Crumb Mixture
1½ cups all-purpose flour
1 cup uncooked old-fashioned oats
¾ cup butter, melted
½ cup sugar
2 teaspoons almond extract
½ teaspoon baking soda
¼ teaspoon salt

Filling
¾ cup peach preserves
⅓ cup flaked coconut

1. Preheat oven to 350°F. Grease 9-inch square baking pan.

2. Combine flour, oats, butter, sugar, almond extract, baking soda and salt in large bowl. Beat with electric mixer at low speed 1 to 2 minutes until mixture is crumbly. Reserve ¾ cup crumb mixture; press remaining crumb mixture onto bottom of prepared baking pan.

3. Spread peach preserves to within ½ inch of edge of crumb mixture; sprinkle reserved crumb mixture and coconut over top. Bake 22 to 27 minutes or until edges are lightly browned. Cool completely. Cut into bars.   *Makes 2 to 2½ dozen bars*

A cookie like a good friend makes the load a little lighter and the laughter a little harder.

Apple Lemon Bars

    Cookie Crust (recipe follows)
1 cup diced, peeled Washington Golden Delicious apple
⅓ cup sugar
1 egg, beaten
2 tablespoons butter or margarine, melted
2 teaspoons grated lemon peel
¾ cup all-purpose flour
¼ teaspoon ground cinnamon
¼ teaspoon baking powder
¼ teaspoon salt
    Lemon Glaze (recipe follows)

Preheat oven to 350°F. Prepare Cookie Crust. Combine apples, sugar, egg, butter and lemon peel in large bowl; mix thoroughly. Combine flour, cinnamon, baking powder and salt in medium bowl; mix well. Stir flour mixture into apple mixture. Spread evenly over crust. Bake 25 minutes or until apples are tender. Cool in pan on wire rack. Brush with Lemon Glaze. *Makes 16 bars*

Cookie Crust: Beat ½ cup butter or margarine, ¼ cup powdered sugar and 2 teaspoons grated lemon peel until creamy; blend in 1 cup flour. Press into bottom of *ungreased* 8-inch square baking pan. Bake at 350°F 15 to 18 minutes or until lightly browned.

Lemon Glaze: Combine ¾ cup powdered sugar and 1 tablespoon lemon juice; mix thoroughly.

Favorite recipe from **Washington Apple Commission**

Pumpkin Harvest Bars

1¾ cups all-purpose flour
  2 teaspoons baking powder
  1 teaspoon grated orange peel
  1 teaspoon ground cinnamon
  ½ teaspoon salt
  ½ teaspoon ground nutmeg
  ¼ teaspoon ground ginger
  ¼ teaspoon ground cloves
  ¾ cup sugar
  ½ cup MOTT'S® Natural Apple Sauce
  ½ cup solid-pack pumpkin
  1 whole egg
  1 egg white
  2 tablespoons vegetable oil
  ½ cup raisins

1. Preheat oven to 350°F. Spray 13×9-inch baking pan with nonstick cooking spray.

2. In small bowl, combine flour, baking powder, orange peel, cinnamon, salt, nutmeg, ginger and cloves.

3. In large bowl, combine sugar, apple sauce, pumpkin, whole egg, egg white and oil.

4. Add flour mixture to apple sauce mixture; stir until well blended. Stir in raisins. Spread batter into prepared pan.

5. Bake 25 to 30 minutes or until toothpick inserted into center comes out clean. Cool on wire rack 15 minutes; cut into 16 bars.

Makes 16 bars

Butterscotch Brownies

2 eggs
2 cups firmly packed brown sugar
½ Butter Flavor CRISCO® Stick or ½ cup Butter Flavor
    CRISCO® all-vegetable shortening, melted, plus
    additional for greasing
1 teaspoon vanilla
1½ cups all-purpose flour
2 teaspoons baking powder
½ teaspoon salt
1 cup finely chopped walnuts or pecans

1. Heat oven to 350°F. Grease 13×9×2-inch pan with shortening. Place cooling rack on countertop.

2. Beat eggs in large bowl at medium speed with electric mixer until light and foamy. Add brown sugar, shortening and vanilla. Beat until creamy.

3. Combine flour, baking powder and salt. Add gradually to egg mixture at low speed until blended. Mix in walnuts. (Dough will be stiff.) Spread in prepared pan.

4. Bake for 25 to 30 minutes or until top is light brown and toothpick inserted into center comes out clean. Cool 10 to 15 minutes on cooling rack. Cut into bars about 2½×2 inches.

Makes 2 dozen bars

Spiced Date Bars

Prep Time: 15 minutes
Bake Time: 30 minutes

½ **cup margarine, softened**
1 **cup packed brown sugar**
2 **eggs**
¾ **cup light sour cream**
2 **cups all-purpose flour**
1 **teaspoon baking soda**
1 **teaspoon ground cinnamon**
½ **teaspoon ground nutmeg**
1 **package (8 or 10 ounces) DOLE® Chopped Dates or Pitted**
    Dates, chopped
    Powdered sugar (optional)

• Beat margarine and brown sugar until light and fluffy. Beat in eggs, one at a time. Stir in sour cream.

• Combine dry ingredients. Beat into sour cream, stir in dates. Spread batter evenly into greased 13×9-inch baking pan.

• Bake at 350°F 25 to 30 minutes or until toothpick inserted into center comes out clean. Cool completely in pan on wire rack. Cut into bars. Dust with powdered sugar.   *Makes 24 bars*

Apple Crumb Squares

  2 cups QUAKER® Oats (quick or old fashioned, uncooked)
1½ cups all-purpose flour
  1 cup packed brown sugar
  ¾ cup (12 tablespoons) butter or margarine, melted
  1 teaspoon ground cinnamon
  ½ teaspoon baking soda
  ½ teaspoon salt (optional)
  ¼ teaspoon ground nutmeg
  1 cup applesauce
  ½ cup chopped nuts

Preheat oven to 350°F. In large bowl, combine all ingredients except applesauce and nuts; mix until crumbly. Reserve 1 cup oats mixture. Press remaining mixture on bottom of greased 13×9-inch metal baking pan. Bake 13 to 15 minutes; cool. Spread applesauce over partially baked crust. Sprinkle reserved 1 cup oats mixture over top; sprinkle with nuts. Bake 13 to 15 minutes or until golden brown. Cool in pan on wire rack; cut into 2-inch squares.

Makes about 2 dozen bars

Walnut Brandy Shortbread

1 **cup butter, softened**
½ **cup firmly packed brown sugar**
⅛ **teaspoon salt**
2 **tablespoons brandy**
1 **cup all-purpose flour**
1 **cup finely chopped toasted California walnuts**
   Granulated sugar

Cream butter with brown sugar and salt in large bowl; mix in brandy. Gradually add flour; stir in walnuts. Spread in *ungreased* 9-inch square baking pan. Refrigerate 30 minutes.

Pierce dough all over with fork. Bake at 325°F about 55 minutes or until dark golden brown. If dough puffs up during baking, pierce again with fork. Sprinkle lightly with granulated sugar; cool. Cut into squares with sharp knife. *Makes 36 squares*

Note: Shortbread may be stored in airtight container at room temperature 1 to 2 months.

Favorite recipe from **Walnut Marketing Board**

Apple Oatmeal Snack Bars

1½ **cups all-purpose flour**
¾ **cup uncooked oats**
1 **teaspoon baking powder**
½ **teaspoon salt**
1 **cup granulated sugar**
2 **tablespoons margarine, softened**
½ **cup MOTT'S® Cinnamon Apple Sauce**
1 **egg**
1 **teaspoon vanilla extract**
1 **cup MOTT'S® Chunky Apple Sauce**
⅓ **cup raisins**
1 **tablespoon firmly packed light brown sugar**
½ **teaspoon ground cinnamon**

1. Preheat oven to 375°F. Spray 8-inch square baking pan with nonstick cooking spray.

2. In medium bowl, combine flour, oats, baking powder and salt.

3. In large bowl, beat granulated sugar and margarine with electric mixer at medium speed until blended. Whisk in ½ cup cinnamon apple sauce, egg and vanilla.

4. Add flour mixture to apple sauce mixture; stir until well blended. Spoon half of batter into prepared pan, spreading evenly.

5. In small bowl, combine 1 cup chunky apple sauce, raisins, brown sugar and cinnamon. Pour evenly over batter.

6. Spoon remaining batter over filling, spreading evenly.

7. Bake 30 to 35 minutes or until lightly browned. Cool on wire rack 15 minutes; cut into 16 bars. *Makes 16 bars*

West Haven Date Bars

   1 cup boiling water
   1 cup chopped pitted dates
   ½ cup (1 stick) butter, softened
   1 cup sugar
   2 eggs
   1 teaspoon vanilla
1½ cups all-purpose flour
   2 tablespoons unsweetened cocoa powder
   1 teaspoon baking soda
   1 cup (6 ounces) semisweet chocolate chips
   ½ cup chopped walnuts or pecans

Preheat oven to 350°F. Lightly grease 13×9-inch pan. Pour boiling water over dates in small bowl; let stand until cooled. Cream butter with sugar in large bowl. Add eggs and vanilla; beat until light. Blend in flour, cocoa and baking soda to make a smooth dough. Stir in date mixture. Spread batter evenly in prepared pan. Sprinkle chocolate chips and nuts over the top. Bake 25 to 30 minutes or just until center feels firm. Cut into 2×1½-inch bars while still warm.

Makes about 3 dozen bars

Zesty Fresh Lemon Bars

Crust
- ½ cup butter or margarine, softened
- ½ cup granulated sugar
- Grated peel of ½ SUNKIST® lemon
- 1¼ cups all-purpose flour

Filling
- 1 cup packed brown sugar
- 1 cup chopped walnuts
- 2 eggs, slightly beaten
- ¼ cup all-purpose flour
- Grated peel of ½ SUNKIST® lemon
- ¼ teaspoon baking powder

Glaze
- 1 cup powdered sugar
- 1 tablespoon butter or margarine, softened
- 2 tablespoons fresh-squeezed SUNKIST® lemon juice

To prepare crust, preheat oven to 350°F. In medium bowl, beat ½ cup butter, granulated sugar and lemon peel. Gradually stir in 1¼ cups flour to form soft dough. Press evenly on bottom of *ungreased* 13×9×2-inch pan. Bake 15 minutes.

To prepare filling, in medium bowl, combine all filling ingredients. Spread over baked crust. Bake 20 minutes. Meanwhile, prepare glaze.

To prepare glaze, in small bowl, gradually blend small amount of powdered sugar into 1 tablespoon butter. Add lemon juice and remaining powdered sugar; stir to blend well. Drizzle glaze over hot lemon filling. Cool in pan on wire rack; cut into bars. Store tightly covered at room temperature.   *Makes about 3 dozen bars*

Apple Date Nut Blondies

2 medium Granny Smith or other firm, tart cooking apples, peeled, cored and finely chopped

2½ cups all-purpose flour, divided

¾ Butter Flavor CRISCO® Stick or ¾ cup Butter Flavor CRISCO® all-vegetable shortening plus additional for greasing

1 cup firmly packed light brown sugar

2 eggs

2 tablespoons vanilla

2 teaspoons baking powder

½ teaspoon salt

½ cup finely chopped pecans

½ cup finely chopped dates

Confectioners' sugar

1. Heat oven to 350°F. Grease 15×10×1-inch jelly-roll pan with shortening. Place cooling rack on countertop.

2. Toss apples with ¼ cup flour.

3. Place shortening and brown sugar in large bowl. Beat at medium speed of electric mixer until well blended. Beat in eggs and vanilla.

4. Combine remaining 2¼ cups flour, baking powder and salt. Add gradually to creamed mixture at low speed. Beat until well blended. Fold in apple mixture, nuts and dates. Spread in greased pan.

5. Bake at 350°F for 25 to 30 minutes or until toothpick inserted into center comes out clean. *Do not overbake.* Remove pan to cooling rack. Cool completely. Cut into bars about 2½×1½ inches. Serve immediately or refrigerate. Dust with confectioners' sugar just before serving. *Makes about 3 dozen bars*

Chocolate Edged Lace Cookies

⅔ **cup ground almonds**
½ **cup (1 stick) butter**
½ **cup sugar**
2 **tablespoons milk**
1 **tablespoon flour**
4 **ounces dark sweet or bittersweet chocolate candy bar, broken into pieces**

Preheat oven to 325°F. Lightly grease cookie sheets. Combine almonds, butter, sugar, milk and flour in large skillet. Cook and stir over low heat until blended. Keep mixture warm over very low heat while forming and baking cookies.

Drop tablespoonfuls of batter 2 inches apart onto prepared cookie sheets. Bake 6 minutes or until golden brown. Cool on cookie sheets 30 seconds to 1 minute before loosening with thin spatula. (If cookies become too brittle, warm briefly in oven.) Remove cookies to wire rack;* cool.

Melt chocolate in small, heavy saucepan over low heat, stirring constantly. Tilt saucepan to pool chocolate at one end; dip edge of each cookie in chocolate, turning cookie slowly so entire edge is tinged with chocolate. Let cookies stand on waxed paper until chocolate is set.

Makes about 2 dozen cookies

*For tuile-shaped cookies, balance wooden spoon over two cans of same height. Working quickly with hot cookies, drape cookies (bottom side down) over handle of spoon so that sides hang down and form taco shape. When firm, transfer to wire rack to cool completely. Dip edges of cooled cookies into chocolate.

Butter Pecan Crisps

  1 cup (2 sticks) unsalted butter, softened
  ¾ cup granulated sugar
  ¾ cup packed brown sugar
  ½ teaspoon salt
  2 eggs
  1 teaspoon vanilla
1½ cups finely ground pecans
2½ cups sifted all-purpose flour
  1 teaspoon baking soda
30 pecan halves
  4 squares (1 ounce each) semisweet chocolate
  1 tablespoon shortening

1. Preheat oven to 375°F. Beat butter, sugars and salt in large bowl until light and fluffy. Add eggs, 1 at a time, beating well after each addition. Beat in vanilla and ground pecans. Combine flour and baking soda in small bowl. Gradually stir flour mixture into butter mixture.

2. Spoon dough into large pastry bag fitted with ⅜-inch round tip; fill bag halfway. Shake down dough to remove air bubbles. Hold bag perpendicular to, and about ½ inch above, parchment paper-lined cookie sheets. Pipe dough into 1¼-inch balls, spacing 3 inches apart. Cut each pecan half lengthwise into 2 slivers. Press 1 sliver in center of each dough ball.

3. Bake 9 to 12 minutes or until lightly browned. Cool 5 minutes on cookie sheets. Remove to wire racks; cool completely. Melt chocolate and shortening in small heavy saucepan over low heat; stir to blend. Drizzle chocolate mixture over cookies. Let stand until chocolate is set. *Makes about 5 dozen cookies*

Almond Tea Cookies

1 **Butter Flavor CRISCO® Stick or 1 cup Butter Flavor CRISCO® all-vegetable shortening**
2 **tablespoons milk**
1 **teaspoon almond extract**
½ **cup granulated sugar**
1⅔ **cups all-purpose flour**
⅔ **cup chopped slivered almonds**
¼ **teaspoon salt**
   Confectioners' sugar

1. Heat oven to 350°F. Place sheets of foil on countertop for cooling cookies.

2. Combine shortening, milk and almond extract in large bowl. Beat at medium speed with electric mixer until well blended. Beat in granulated sugar.

3. Combine flour, almonds and salt. Add gradually to creamed mixture at low speed. Shape dough into balls using 1 level measuring tablespoon for each. Place 2 inches apart on *ungreased* baking sheet.

4. Bake for 10 to 12 minutes or until set. Cookies will not brown. *Do not overbake.* Cool 2 minutes on baking sheet. Remove cookies to foil to cool completely.

5. Roll slightly warm cookies in confectioners' sugar. Roll in confectioners' sugar again when cookies are cool.

Makes 3 dozen cookies

Chocolate-Flecked Pirouettes

½ cup (1 stick) butter, softened
½ cup sugar
 2 egg whites
 1 teaspoon vanilla
½ cup all-purpose flour
⅓ cup coarsely grated bittersweet or dark sweet chocolate
    bar (about 2 ounces)

1. Preheat oven to 400°F. Grease cookie sheets well; set aside.

2. Beat butter and sugar in small bowl with electric mixer at medium speed until light and fluffy. Beat in egg whites, 1 at a time. Beat in vanilla. Add flour; beat at low speed just until blended. Gently fold in grated chocolate with rubber spatula.

3. Drop teaspoonfuls of batter 4 inches apart onto prepared cookie sheets. Spread dough into 2-inch rounds with small spatula. Make only 3 to 4 rounds per sheet.

4. Bake 1 sheet at a time 4 to 5 minutes until edges are barely golden. *Do not overbake.*

5. Remove from oven and quickly loosen edge of 1 cookie from baking sheet with thin spatula. Quickly roll cookie around clean handle of wooden spoon overlapping edges to form cigar shape. Repeat with remaining cookies. (If cookies become too firm to shape, return to oven for a few seconds to soften.) Slide cookie off handle to wire rack; cool completely.

6. Store tightly covered at room temperature or freeze up to 3 months.   *Makes about 3 dozen cookies*

Pecan Tassies

Crust
- 1 package (3 ounces) cream cheese
- ½ Butter Flavor CRISCO® Stick or ½ cup Butter Flavor CRISCO® all-vegetable shortening
- 1 cup all-purpose flour

Filling
- 1 egg, lightly beaten
- ¾ cup firmly packed brown sugar
- 1 tablespoon Butter Flavor CRISCO® Stick or 1 tablespoon Butter Flavor CRISCO® all-vegetable shortening
- 1 teaspoon vanilla
- ⅔ cup pecan pieces

1. For crust, combine cream cheese and shortening in medium bowl. Beat at medium speed with electric mixer until blended. Add flour gradually at low speed. Mix until well blended. Cover. Chill at least 2 hours.

2. Heat oven to 350°F. Place sheets of foil on countertop for cooling cookies.

3. Shape dough into 2 dozen 1-inch balls. Press balls onto bottom and all the way up sides to top edge of *ungreased* 1¾-inch muffin cups.

4. For filling, combine egg, brown sugar, 1 tablespoon shortening and vanilla in medium bowl. Stir until well mixed. Stir in pecans. Fill each cup ¾ full. *Do not overfill.*

5. Bake for 25 minutes. *Do not overbake.* Cool 10 minutes in pan. Remove carefully. Remove cookies to foil to cool completely.

Makes 2 dozen tarts

Cook's Tip: If 1¾-inch muffin cups are not available, Pecan Tassies can be baked in *ungreased* regular 2½-inch muffin cups. Divide dough into 12 equal balls. Press balls onto bottom and up sides to ¼ inch from top. Fill each cup ¾ full. *Do not overfill.* Bake at 350°F for 30 minutes. Cool as above. Makes 1 dozen tarts.

Almond Cream Cheese Cookies

　1 (3-ounce) package cream cheese, softened
　1 cup butter, softened
　1 cup sugar
　1 egg yolk
　1 tablespoon milk
　⅛ teaspoon almond extract
2½ cups sifted cake flour
　1 cup BLUE DIAMOND® Sliced Natural Almonds, toasted

Beat cream cheese with butter and sugar until fluffy. Blend in egg yolk, milk and almond extract. Gradually mix in flour. Gently stir in almonds. (Dough will be sticky.) Divide dough in half; place each half on large sheet of waxed paper. Working through waxed paper, shape each half into 12×1½-inch roll. Chill until very firm.

Preheat oven to 325°F. Cut rolls into ¼-inch slices. Bake on *ungreased* cookie sheets 10 to 15 minutes or until edges are golden. (Cookies will not brown.) Cool on wire racks.　　　　*Makes about 4 dozen cookies*

Almond Lace Cookies

¼ cup butter, softened
½ cup sugar
½ cup BLUE DIAMOND® Blanched Almond Paste
¼ cup all-purpose flour
¼ teaspoon salt
½ teaspoon almond extract
2 tablespoons milk
2 teaspoons grated orange peel

Cream butter and sugar. Beat in almond paste. Add remaining ingredients. Mix well. Drop rounded teaspoonfuls onto cookie sheet, 3 inches apart. (Cookies will spread.) Bake at 350°F for 8 to 10 minutes or until edges are lightly browned. Cool 3 to 4 minutes on cookie sheet; remove and cool on wire rack.

Makes 1½ dozen cookies

Chocolate-Dipped Coconut Macaroons

Prep Time: 15 minutes
Bake Time: 20 minutes

**1 package (14 ounces) BAKER'S® ANGEL FLAKE® Coconut
(5⅓ cups)**
⅔ cup sugar
6 tablespoons flour
¼ teaspoon salt
4 egg whites
1 teaspoon almond extract
**1 package (8 squares) BAKER'S® Semi-Sweet Baking
Chocolate, melted**

HEAT oven to 325°F.

MIX coconut, sugar, flour and salt in large bowl. Stir in egg whites
and almond extract until well blended. Drop by teaspoonfuls onto
greased and floured cookie sheets.

BAKE 20 minutes or until edges of cookies are golden brown.
Immediately remove from cookie sheets to wire racks and cool
completely. Dip cookies halfway into melted chocolate. Let stand at
room temperature or refrigerate on wax paper-lined tray 30 minutes
or until chocolate is firm.   *Makes about 3 dozen cookies*

Cook's Tip: Store in tightly covered container up to 1 week.

Date Pinwheel Cookies

1¼ **cups dates, pitted and finely chopped**
¾ **cup orange juice**
½ **cup granulated sugar**
1 **tablespoon butter**
3 **cups plus 1 tablespoon all-purpose flour, divided**
2 **teaspoons vanilla, divided**
4 **ounces cream cheese**
¼ **cup shortening**
1 **cup packed brown sugar**
2 **eggs**
1 **teaspoon baking soda**
½ **teaspoon salt**

1. Heat dates, orange juice, granulated sugar, butter and 1 tablespoon flour in medium saucepan over medium heat. Cook 10 minutes or until thick, stirring frequently; remove from heat. Stir in 1 teaspoon vanilla; set aside to cool.

2. Beat cream cheese, shortening and brown sugar about 3 minutes in large bowl until light and fluffy. Add eggs and remaining 1 teaspoon vanilla; beat 2 minutes longer.

3. Combine remaining 3 cups flour, baking soda and salt in medium bowl. Add to shortening mixture; stir just until blended. Divide dough in half. Roll one half of dough on lightly floured surface into 12×9-inch rectangle. Spread half of date mixture over dough. Spread evenly, leaving ¼-inch border at top short edge. Starting at short side, tightly roll up dough jelly-roll style. Wrap in plastic wrap; freeze for at least 1 hour. Repeat with remaining dough.

4. Preheat oven to 350°F. Grease cookie sheets. Unwrap dough. Using heavy thread or dental floss, cut dough into ¼-inch slices. Place slices 1 inch apart on prepared cookie sheets.

5. Bake 12 minutes or until lightly browned. Let cookies stand on cookie sheets 2 minutes. Remove cookies to wire racks; cool completely. *Makes 6 dozen cookies*

Chocolate Madeleines

1¼ cups all-purpose flour
1 cup sugar
⅛ teaspoon salt
¾ cup (1½ sticks) butter, melted (no substitutes)
⅓ cup HERSHEY'S Cocoa
3 eggs
2 egg yolks
½ teaspoon vanilla extract
Chocolate Frosting (recipe follows)

1. Heat oven to 350°F. Lightly grease indentations of madeleine mold pan (each shell is 3×2 inches).

2. Stir together flour, sugar and salt in medium saucepan. Combine melted butter and cocoa; stir into dry ingredients. In small bowl, lightly beat eggs, egg yolks and vanilla with fork until well blended; stir into chocolate mixture, blending well. Cook over very low heat, stirring constantly, until mixture is warm. Do not simmer or boil. Remove from heat. Fill each mold half full with batter. (Do not overfill.)

3. Bake 8 to 10 minutes or until wooden toothpick inserted into centers comes out clean. Invert onto wire rack; cool completely. Prepare Chocolate Frosting; frost flat sides of cookies. Press frosted sides together, forming shells.   *Makes about 1½ dozen filled cookies*

Chocolate Frosting

1¼ cups powdered sugar
2 tablespoons HERSHEY'S Cocoa
2 tablespoons butter, softened (no substitutes)
2 to 2½ tablespoons milk
½ teaspoon vanilla extract

Stir together powdered sugar and cocoa in small bowl. In another small bowl, beat butter and ¼ cup of the cocoa mixture until fluffy. Gradually add remaining cocoa mixture alternately with milk, beating to spreading consistency. Stir in vanilla.

Classic Anise Biscotti

    4 ounces whole blanched almonds (about ¾ cup)
2¼ cups all-purpose flour
    1 teaspoon baking powder
    ¾ teaspoon salt
    ¾ cup sugar
    ½ cup (1 stick) unsalted butter, softened
    3 eggs
    2 tablespoons brandy
    2 teaspoons grated lemon peel
    1 tablespoon whole anise seeds

1. Preheat oven to 375°F. To toast almonds, spread almonds on baking sheet. Bake 6 to 8 minutes or until toasted and light brown; turn off oven. Remove almonds with spoon to cutting board; cool. Coarsely chop almonds.

2. Combine flour, baking powder and salt in small bowl. Beat sugar and butter in medium bowl with electric mixer at medium speed until light and fluffy. Add eggs, 1 at a time, beating well after each addition and scraping side of bowl often. Stir in brandy and lemon peel. Add flour mixture gradually; stir until smooth. Stir in chopped almonds and anise seeds. Cover and refrigerate dough 1 hour or until firm.

3. Preheat oven to 375°F. Grease large baking sheet. Divide dough in half. Shape ½ of dough into 12×2-inch log on lightly floured surface. (Dough will be fairly soft.) Pat smooth with lightly floured fingertips. Transfer to prepared baking sheet. Repeat with remaining ½ of dough to form second log. Bake 20 to 25 minutes or until logs are light golden brown. Remove baking sheet from oven to wire rack; turn off oven. Cool logs completely.

4. Preheat oven to 350°F. Cut logs diagonally with serrated knife into ½-inch-thick slices. Place slices flat in single layer on 2 *ungreased* baking sheets.

5. Bake 8 minutes. Turn slices over; bake 10 to 12 minutes or until cut surfaces are light brown and cookies are dry. Remove cookies to wire racks; cool completely. Store cookies in airtight container up to 2 weeks.   *Makes about 4 dozen cookies*

Chocolate Macaroon Squares

  1 package (18.25 ounce) chocolate cake mix
  ⅓ cup butter or margarine, softened
  1 large egg, lightly beaten
  1 can (14 ounces) **NESTLÉ® CARNATION®** Sweetened
     Condensed Milk
  1 large egg
  1 teaspoon vanilla extract
1⅓ cups flaked sweetened coconut, *divided*
  1 cup chopped pecans
  1 cup (6-ounce package) **NESTLÉ® TOLL HOUSE®**
     Semi-Sweet Chocolate Morsels

PREHEAT oven to 350°F.

COMBINE cake mix, butter and egg in large bowl; mix with fork until crumbly. Press onto bottom of *ungreased* 13×9-inch baking pan. Combine sweetened condensed milk, egg and vanilla extract in medium bowl; beat until well blended. Stir in *1 cup* coconut, nuts and morsels.

SPREAD mixture evenly over base; sprinkle with remaining coconut. Bake for 28 to 30 minutes or until center is almost set (center will firm when cool). Cool in pan on wire rack.   *Makes 24 squares*

Nothing tastes as good as the last cookie.

Espresso Shortbread Bars

**1 Butter Flavor CRISCO® Stick or 1cup Butter Flavor
CRISCO® all-vegetable shortening**
½ cup firmly packed light brown sugar
1 teaspoon vanilla
1 teaspoon instant coffee
2¼ cups all-purpose flour
¼ teaspoon salt

1. Combine shortening and sugar in large bowl. Beat at medium speed with electric mixer until well blended. Beat in vanilla and instant coffee until instant coffee is dissolved and mixture is fluffy.

2. Combine flour and salt in small bowl. Add to creamed mixture until well blended. Refrigerate dough 4 hours or overnight.

3. Heat the oven to 325°F.

4. Spray cookie sheets with CRISCO® No-Stick Cooking Spray. Roll dough out to ¼ inch thick. Cut dough into rectangular bars 3×1-inches long; prick tops with fork and place on prepared cookie sheets. Bake at 325°F for 20 to 25 minutes or until golden. Cool on cookie sheets 4 minutes; transfer to cooling racks.

Makes about 3 dozen bars

Double-Dipped Hazelnut Crisps

¾ **cup semisweet chocolate chips**
1¼ **cups all-purpose flour**
¾ **cup powdered sugar**
⅔ **cup whole hazelnuts, toasted, hulled and finely ground***
¼ **teaspoon instant espresso powder**
   Dash salt
½ **cup (1 stick) butter, softened**
 2 **teaspoons vanilla**
 4 **squares (1 ounce each) bittersweet or semisweet**
   chocolate
 2 **teaspoons shortening, divided**
 4 **ounces white chocolate**

*To grind hazelnuts, place in food processor or blender. Process until thoroughly ground with a dry, not pasty, texture.

1. Preheat oven to 350°F. Lightly grease cookie sheets or line with parchment paper. Melt chocolate chips in top of double boiler over hot, not boiling, water. Remove from heat; cool. Blend flour, powdered sugar, hazelnuts, espresso powder and salt in large bowl. Blend in butter, melted chocolate and vanilla until dough is stiff but smooth. (If dough is too soft to handle, cover and refrigerate until firm.)

2. Roll out dough, ¼ at a time, to ⅛-inch thickness on lightly floured surface. Cut with 2-inch scalloped round cutters. Place 2 inches apart on prepared cookie sheets. Bake 8 minutes or until not quite firm. (Cookies should not brown. They will puff up during baking and then flatten again.) Remove to wire racks to cool.

3. Place bittersweet chocolate and 1 teaspoon shortening in small bowl. Place bowl over hot water; stir until chocolate is melted and smooth. Dip cookies, 1 at a time, halfway into bittersweet chocolate. Place on waxed paper; refrigerate until chocolate is set. Repeat melting process with white chocolate. Dip plain halves of cookies into white chocolate; refrigerate until set. Store cookies in airtight container in cool place. (If cookies are frozen, chocolate might discolor.)
Makes about 4 dozen cookies

Maple Pecan Sandwich Cookies

Cookies
- 1¼ cups firmly packed light brown sugar
- 1 Butter Flavor CRISCO® Stick or 1 cup Butter Flavor CRISCO® all-vegetable shortening
- 2 eggs
- ¼ cup maple syrup or maple-flavored pancake syrup
- 1 teaspoon maple extract
- ½ teaspoon vanilla
- 2½ cups all-purpose flour plus 4 tablespoons, divided
- 1½ cups finely ground pecans
- ¾ teaspoon baking powder
- ½ teaspoon baking soda
- ½ teaspoon salt
- 20 to 30 pecan halves (optional)

Filling
- 1¼ cups confectioners' sugar
- 3 tablespoons Butter Flavor CRISCO® Stick or 3 tablespoons Butter Flavor CRISCO® all-vegetable shortening
- 1 teaspoon maple extract
- Dash salt
- 2½ teaspoons milk

1. For cookies, place brown sugar and shortening in large bowl. Beat at medium speed of electric mixer until well blended. Add eggs, syrup, maple extract and vanilla; beat until well blended and fluffy.

2. Combine 2½ cups flour, ground pecans, baking powder, baking soda and salt. Add gradually to shortening mixture, beating at low speed until well blended. Divide dough into 4 equal pieces; shape each into disk. Wrap with plastic wrap. Refrigerate 1 hour or until firm.

3. Heat oven to 375°F. Place sheets of foil on countertop for cooling cookies.

4. Sprinkle about 1 tablespoon flour on large sheet of waxed paper. Place disk of dough on floured paper; flatten slightly with hands. Turn

dough over; cover with another large sheet of waxed paper. Roll dough to ¼-inch thickness. Cut out with floured 3-inch scalloped round cookie cutter. Place 2 inches apart on *ungreased* baking sheet. Roll out remaining dough. Place pecans in center of half of cookies, if desired.

5. Bake one baking sheet at a time at 375°F for 5 to 7 minutes or until lightly browned around edges. *Do not overbake.* Cool 2 minutes on baking sheet. Remove cookies to foil to cool completely.

6. For filling, place confectioners' sugar, shortening, maple extract and salt in medium bowl. Beat at low speed until smooth. Add milk; beat until mixture is smooth. Spread filling on flat side of 1 plain cookie. Cover with flat side of second cookie with pecan. Repeat with remaining cookies and filling.   *Makes about 2 dozen sandwich cookies*

Chocolate-Dipped Almond Crescents

   1 cup (2 sticks) butter, softened
   1 cup powdered sugar
   2 egg yolks
   2½ cups all-purpose flour
   1½ teaspoons almond extract
   1 cup (6 ounces) semisweet chocolate chips

1. Preheat oven to 375°F. Line cookie sheets with parchment paper or leave *ungreased*.

2. Cream butter, sugar and egg yolks in large bowl. Beat in flour and almond extract until well mixed. Shape dough into 1-inch balls. (If dough is too soft to handle, cover and refrigerate until firm.) Roll balls into 2-inch-long ropes, tapering both ends. Curve ropes into crescent shapes.

3. Place 2 inches apart on cookie sheets. Bake 8 to 10 minutes or until set, but not browned. Remove to wire racks to cool. Melt chocolate chips in top of double boiler over hot, not boiling, water. Dip one end of each crescent in melted chocolate. Place on waxed paper; cool until chocolate is set.   *Makes about 5 dozen cookies*

Almond Biscotti

¼ **cup finely chopped slivered almonds**
½ **cup sugar**
2 **tablespoons margarine**
4 **egg whites, lightly beaten**
2 **teaspoons almond extract**
2 **cups all-purpose flour**
2 **teaspoons baking powder**
¼ **teaspoon salt**

1. Preheat oven to 375°F. Place almonds in small baking pan. Bake 7 to 8 minutes or until golden brown. (Watch almonds carefully. They burn easily.) Set aside.

2. Beat sugar and margarine in medium bowl with electric mixer until smooth. Add egg whites and almond extract; mix well. Combine flour, baking powder and salt in large bowl; mix well. Stir egg white mixture and almonds into flour mixture until well blended.

3. Spray two 9×5-inch loaf pans with nonstick cooking spray. Evenly divide dough between prepared pans; spread dough evenly onto bottoms of pans with wet fingertips. Bake 15 minutes or until knife inserted into centers comes out clean. Remove from oven; turn out onto cutting board.

4. As soon as loaves are cool enough to handle, cut each loaf into 16 (½-inch-thick) slices. Place slices on baking sheets covered with parchment paper or sprayed with cooking spray. Bake 5 minutes; turn over. Bake 5 minutes more or until golden brown. Serve warm or cool completely and store in airtight container. *Makes 32 biscotti*

Peanut Butter Kisses

1¼ cups firmly packed light brown sugar
¾ cup creamy peanut butter
½ CRISCO® Stick or ½ cup CRISCO® all-vegetable
   shortening
3 tablespoons milk
1 tablespoon vanilla
1 egg
1¾ cups all-purpose flour
¾ teaspoon baking soda
¾ teaspoon salt
48 chocolate kisses, unwrapped

1. Heat oven to 375°F. Place sheets of foil on countertop for cooling cookies.

2. Combine brown sugar, peanut butter, shortening, milk and vanilla in large bowl. Beat at medium speed of electric mixer until well blended. Add egg. Beat just until blended.

3. Combine flour, baking soda and salt. Add to shortening mixture; beat at low speed until just blended.

4. Form dough into 1-inch balls. Roll in granulated sugar. Place 2 inches apart on *ungreased* baking sheets.

5. Bake one baking sheet at a time at 375°F for 6 minutes. Press chocolate kiss into center of each cookie. Return to oven. Bake 3 minutes. *Do not overbake.* Cool 2 minutes on baking sheets. Remove cookies to foil to cool completely.   *Makes about 3 dozen cookies*

Pecan Florentines

¾ cup pecan halves, finely ground*
½ cup all-purpose flour
⅓ cup packed brown sugar
¼ cup light corn syrup
¼ cup (½ stick) butter
2 tablespoons milk
⅓ cup semisweet chocolate chips

*To grind pecans, place in food processor or blender. Process until thoroughly ground with a dry, not pasty, texture.

1. Preheat oven to 350°F. Line cookie sheets with foil; lightly grease foil. Combine pecans and flour in small bowl. Combine brown sugar, syrup, butter and milk in medium saucepan. Stir over medium heat until mixture comes to a boil. Remove from heat; stir in flour mixture.

2. Drop by teaspoonfuls about 3 inches apart onto prepared cookie sheets. Bake 10 to 12 minutes or until lacy and golden brown. (Cookies are soft when hot, but become crisp as they cool.) Cool completely on foil.

3. Place chocolate chips in small resealable plastic food storage bag; seal. Microwave at HIGH 1 minute. Knead bag lightly. Repeat steps as necessary until chips are completely melted. With scissors, snip off small corner from one side of bag. Squeeze melted chocolate over cookies to decorate. Let stand until chocolate is set. Peel cookies off foil.

Makes about 3 dozen cookies

Mini Lemon Sandwich Cookies

Cookies
  2 **cups all-purpose flour**
  1 **cup (2 sticks) butter, softened**
  ⅓ **cup whipping cream**
  ¼ **cup granulated sugar**
  1 **teaspoon lemon peel**
  ⅛ **teaspoon lemon extract**
  Granulated sugar for dipping

Filling
  ¾ **cup powdered sugar**
  ¼ **cup (½ stick) butter, softened**
  1 **to 3 teaspoons lemon juice**
  1 **teaspoon vanilla**
  Food coloring (optional)

1. For cookies, combine flour, 1 cup butter, whipping cream, ¼ cup granulated sugar, lemon peel and lemon extract in small bowl. Beat 2 to 3 minutes, scraping bowl often, until well blended. Divide dough into thirds. Wrap each portion in waxed paper; refrigerate until firm.

2. Preheat oven to 375°F. Roll out each portion of dough to ⅛-inch thickness on well-floured surface. Cut out with 1½-inch round cookie cutter. Dip both sides of each cookie in granulated sugar. Place 1 inch apart on *ungreased* cookie sheets. Pierce with fork. Bake 6 to 9 minutes or until slightly puffy but not brown. Cool 1 minute on cookie sheets; remove to wire racks to cool completely.

3. For filling, combine powdered sugar, ¼ cup butter, lemon juice and vanilla in small bowl. Beat 1 to 2 minutes, scraping bowl often, until smooth. Tint with food coloring, if desired. Spread ½ teaspoon filling each on bottoms of ½ the cookies. Top with remaining cookies.

Makes 4½ dozen sandwich cookies

Pecan Praline Cookies

¾ **Butter Flavor CRISCO® Stick or ¾ cup Butter Flavor CRISCO® all-vegetable shortening plus additional for greasing**
1½ **cups firmly packed brown sugar**
  1 **egg**
  1 **teaspoon vanilla**
1½ **cups all-purpose flour**
  1 **cup chopped pecans**

1. Heat oven to 375°F. Grease baking sheet with shortening. Place sheets of foil on countertop for cooling cookies.

2. Combine shortening and brown sugar in large bowl. Beat at medium speed with electric mixer until creamy. Beat in egg and vanilla. Beat until light and fluffy. Add flour and pecans. Stir until well blended.

3. Shape level measuring tablespoons of dough into balls. Flatten to ⅛-inch thickness. Place 1 inch apart on prepared baking sheet.

4. Bake for 7 to 8 minutes or until edges are golden brown. *Do not overbake.* Cool on baking sheet 2 minutes. Remove cookies to foil to cool completely. *Makes 4 dozen cookies*

Orange & Chocolate Ribbon Cookies

1 cup (2 sticks) butter, softened
½ cup sugar
3 egg yolks
2¼ cups all-purpose flour, divided
2 teaspoons grated orange peel
1 teaspoon orange extract
3 tablespoons unsweetened cocoa powder
1 teaspoon vanilla
1 teaspoon chocolate extract

1. Beat butter, sugar and egg yolks in large bowl until light and fluffy. Remove half of mixture; place in another bowl. Add 1¼ cups flour, orange peel and orange extract to one half of mixture; mix until blended and smooth. Shape into a ball. Add cocoa, vanilla and chocolate extract to second half of mixture; beat until smooth. Stir in remaining 1 cup flour; mix until blended and smooth. Shape into a ball. Cover both halves of dough; refrigerate 10 minutes.

2. Roll out each dough separately on lightly floured surface to 12×4-inch rectangle. Pat edges of dough to straighten; use rolling pin to level off thickness. Place one dough on top of the other. Using sharp knife, make lengthwise cut through center of doughs. Lift half of dough onto other to make long, 4-layer strip of dough. With hands, press dough strips together. Wrap in plastic wrap; refrigerate at least 1 hour or up to 3 days. (For longer storage, freeze up to 6 weeks.)

3. Preheat oven to 350°F. Lightly grease cookie sheets or line with parchment paper. Cut dough crosswise into ¼-inch-thick slices; place 2 inches apart on prepared cookie sheets. Bake 10 to 12 minutes or until very lightly browned. Remove to wire racks; cool.

Makes about 5 dozen cookies

Slice 'n' Bake Ginger Wafers

½ cup (1 stick) butter, softened
1 cup packed brown sugar
¼ cup light molasses
1 egg
2 teaspoons ground ginger
1 teaspoon grated orange peel
¼ teaspoon salt
¼ teaspoon ground cinnamon
¼ teaspoon ground cloves
2 cups all-purpose flour

1. Beat butter, sugar and molasses in large bowl until light and fluffy. Add egg, ginger, orange peel, salt, cinnamon and cloves; beat until well blended. Stir in flour until well blended. (Dough will be very stiff.)

2. Divide dough in half. Roll each half into 8×1½-inch log. Wrap logs in waxed paper or plastic wrap; refrigerate at least 5 hours or up to 3 days.

3. Preheat oven to 350°F. Cut dough into ¼-inch-thick slices. Place about 2 inches apart on *ungreased* baking sheets. Bake 12 to 14 minutes or until set. Remove from baking sheets to wire racks to cool.   *Makes about 4½ dozen cookies*

Variation: Dip half of each cookie in melted white chocolate or drizzle cookies with a glaze of 1¼ cups powdered sugar and 2 tablespoons orange juice. Or, cut cookie dough into ⅛-inch-thick slices and bake. Sandwich melted caramel candy or peanut butter between cooled cookies.

Orange Pecan Refrigerator Cookies

2⅓ cups all-purpose flour
½ teaspoon baking soda
¼ teaspoon salt
½ cup butter or margarine, softened
½ cup granulated sugar
½ cup packed brown sugar
1 egg, lightly beaten
Grated peel of 1 SUNKIST® orange
3 tablespoons fresh squeezed SUNKIST® orange juice
¾ cup pecan pieces

In bowl, stir together flour, baking soda and salt. In large bowl, blend together butter, granulated sugar and brown sugar. Add egg, orange peel and juice; beat well. Stir in pecans. Gradually beat in flour mixture. (Dough will be stiff.) Divide mixture in half and shape each half (on long piece of waxed paper) into roll about 1¼ inches in diameter and 12 inches long. Roll up tightly in waxed paper. Chill several hours or overnight.

Cut into ¼-inch slices and arrange on lightly greased cookie sheets. Bake at 350°F for 10 to 12 minutes or until lightly browned. Cool on wire racks. *Makes about 6 dozen cookies*

Chocolate Filled Sandwich Cookies: Cut each roll into ⅛-inch slices and bake as above. When cool, to make each sandwich cookie, spread about 1 teaspoon canned chocolate fudge frosting on bottom side of 1 cookie; cover with second cookie of same shape. Makes about 3 dozen double cookies.

Chocolate Florentines

¼ cup **Candied Orange Peel (recipe page 127)**
½ cup **(1 stick) butter (no substitutes)**
⅔ cup **sugar**
 2 **tablespoons milk**
 2 **tablespoons light corn syrup**
⅓ cup **all-purpose flour**
 1 **cup sliced almonds**
 1 **teaspoon vanilla extract**
   Chocolate Filling (recipe page 127)

1. Prepare Candied Orange Peel.

2. Heat oven to 350°F. Line cookie sheets with heavy duty foil; smooth out wrinkles.

3. Place butter, sugar, milk and corn syrup in medium saucepan. Cook over medium heat, stirring constantly, until mixture boils. Continue cooking, without stirring, until syrup reaches 230°F on candy thermometer or until syrup spins 2-inch thread when dropped from fork or spoon. Remove from heat. Stir in flour, candied orange peel, almonds and vanilla. (To keep mixture from hardening, immediately place pan over hot water.) Drop mixture by level teaspoons onto prepared cookie sheets, placing at least 4 inches apart. (Cookies will spread a great deal during baking.)

4. Bake 8 to 11 minutes or until cookies are bubbly all over and are light brown caramel color. Remove from oven; cool. (Carefully slide foil off cookie sheet to reuse cookie sheet; prepare with foil for next use.) Cool cookies completely on foil; gently peel off foil.

5. Prepare Chocolate Filling; spread thin layer on flat side of one cookie; gently press on another cookie, flat sides together. Wrap individually in plastic wrap. Repeat with remaining cookies and filling. Store tightly covered in refrigerator.

Makes about 1½ dozen filled cookies

Candied Orange Peel: Cut outer peel (no white membrane) of 2 small navel oranges into ½ inch wide strips. Cut across strips to make ½×⅛-inch pieces. In small saucepan, place peel, ¼ cup sugar and ½ cup water. Cook over very low heat until bottom of pan is covered only with glazed peel; do not caramelize. Remove from heat; spoon onto wax paper. Cool.

Chocolate Filling: In small microwave-safe bowl, place 1 cup HERSHEY'S Semi-Sweet Chocolate Chips. Microwave at HIGH (100% power) 1 minute; stir. If necessary, microwave at HIGH an additional 15 seconds at a time, stirring after each heating, just until chips are melted when stirred.

Walnut Meringues

3 **egg whites**
Pinch salt
¾ **cup sugar**
⅓ **cup finely chopped walnuts**

1. Preheat oven to 350°F. Line baking sheet with parchment paper.

2. Place egg whites and salt in large bowl. Beat until soft peaks form. Gradually add sugar, beating until stiff peaks form. Gently fold in walnuts.

3. Drop mounds about 1 inch in diameter 1 inch apart onto prepared baking sheet. Bake 20 minutes or until lightly browned and dry to the touch. Let cool completely before removing from baking sheet. Store in airtight container. *Makes 48 cookies*

Double Almond Butter Cookies

Dough
- 2 cups butter, softened
- 2½ cups powdered sugar, divided
- 4 cups all-purpose flour
- 2 teaspoons vanilla

Filling
- ⅔ cup BLUE DIAMOND® Blanched Almond Paste
- ¼ cup packed light brown sugar
- ½ cup BLUE DIAMOND® Chopped Natural Almonds, toasted
- ¼ teaspoon vanilla

For dough, beat butter and 1 cup powdered sugar until smooth. Gradually beat in flour. Beat in 2 teaspoons vanilla. Chill dough ½ hour.

For filling, combine almond paste, brown sugar, almonds and ¼ teaspoon vanilla.

Preheat oven to 350°F. Shape dough around ½ teaspoon filling mixture to form 1-inch balls. Place on *ungreased* cookie sheets.

Bake 15 minutes. Cool on wire racks. Roll cookies in remaining 1½ cups powdered sugar or sift over cookies.

Makes about 8 dozen cookies

Classic Refrigerator Sugar Cookies

1 cup (2 sticks) butter, softened
1 cup sugar
1 egg
1 teaspoon vanilla
2 cups all-purpose flour
2 teaspoons baking powder
Dash nutmeg
¼ cup milk
Colored sprinkles or melted semisweet chocolate chips*
(optional)

*To dip 24 cookies, melt 1 cup chocolate chips in small saucepan over very low heat until smooth.

1. Beat butter in large bowl with electric mixer at medium speed until smooth. Add sugar; beat until well blended. Add egg and vanilla; beat until well blended.

2. Combine flour, baking powder and nutmeg in medium bowl. Add flour mixture and milk alternately to butter mixture, beating at low speed after each addition until well blended.

3. Shape dough into 2 logs, each about 2 inches in diameter and 6 inches long. Roll logs in colored sprinkles, if desired, coating evenly (about ¼ cup sprinkles per roll). Or, leave logs plain and decorate cookies with melted chocolate after baking. Wrap each log in plastic wrap. Refrigerate 2 to 3 hours or overnight.

4. Preheat oven to 350°F. Grease cookie sheets. Cut logs into ¼-inch-thick slices; place 1 inch apart on prepared cookie sheets. (Keep unbaked logs and sliced cookies chilled until ready to bake.)

5. Bake 8 to 10 minutes or until edges are golden brown. Transfer to wire racks to cool.

6. Dip plain cookies in melted chocolate, or drizzle chocolate over cookies with fork or spoon, if desired. Set cookies on wire racks until chocolate is set. Store in airtight container.

Makes about 4 dozen cookies

Lemon Buttermilk Baby Cakes

½ **cup butter, softened**
1 **cup sugar**
1 **egg**
¾ **cup buttermilk**
1 **tablespoon grated lemon peel**
1 **tablespoon fresh lemon juice**
½ **teaspoon vanilla**
2 **cups plus 2 tablespoons all-purpose flour**
½ **teaspoon baking soda**
½ **teaspoon salt**

Beat butter in large bowl until light and fluffy. Add sugar; beat until well blended. Add egg; mix until well blended. Stir in buttermilk, lemon peel, lemon juice and vanilla. Sift together flour, baking soda and salt in small bowl; gradually add to butter mixture. Chill dough at least 2 hours.

Preheat oven to 400°F. Drop small rounded teaspoons of dough onto lightly greased cookie sheets. Bake 6 to 8 minutes or until edges are lightly browned. Sprinkle pinch of sugar over each cookie; remove to wire racks to cool.   *Makes approximately 5 dozen cookies*

Cook's Tip: Cookie dough can be frozen and baked in small batches when needed.

Favorite recipe from **The Sugar Association, Inc.**

Walnut Macaroons

2⅔ cups flaked coconut
1¼ cups coarsely chopped California walnuts
⅓ cup flour
½ teaspoon ground cinnamon
¼ teaspoon salt
4 egg whites
1 teaspoon grated lemon peel
2 squares (1 ounce each) semisweet chocolate

Combine coconut, walnuts, flour, cinnamon and salt. Add egg whites and lemon peel; mix well.

Drop teaspoonfuls of walnut mixture onto lightly greased baking sheets. Bake in 325°F oven 20 minutes or until golden brown. Remove from baking sheets immediately.

Place chocolate in microwavable bowl. Microwave on HIGH (100% power) until melted, about 2½ minutes; stir. Dip macaroon bottoms in chocolate. Place on waxed paper. Let stand until chocolate is set up.

Makes about 3 dozen cookies

Favorite recipe from **Walnut Marketing Board**

Chocolate-Dipped Almond Horns

  1 can SOLO® Almond Paste
  3 egg whites
  ½ cup sugar
  ½ teaspoon almond extract
  ¼ cup plus 2 tablespoons all-purpose flour
  ½ cup sliced almonds
  5 squares (1 ounce each) semisweet chocolate, melted and
     cooled

Preheat oven to 350°F. Grease 2 cookie sheets; set aside. Break almond paste into small pieces and place in medium bowl or food processor container. Add egg whites, sugar and almond extract. Beat with electric mixer or process until mixture is very smooth. Add flour and beat or process until blended.

Spoon almond mixture into pastry bag fitted with ½-inch (#8) plain tip. Pipe mixture into 5- or 6-inch crescent shapes on prepared cookie sheets, about 1½ inches apart. Sprinkle with sliced almonds.

Bake 13 to 15 minutes or until edges are golden brown. Cool on cookie sheets on wire racks 2 minutes. Remove from cookie sheets and cool completely on wire racks. Dip ends of cookies in melted chocolate and place on aluminum foil. Let stand until chocolate is set.

Makes about 16 cookies

Shortbread Cookies

Prep Time: 15 minutes
Bake Time: 13 minutes

**1½ cups (3 sticks) butter or margarine, softened
  1 package (8 ounces) PHILADELPHIA® Cream Cheese,
    softened
  ½ cup granulated sugar
  3 cups flour
    Powdered sugar**

MIX butter, cream cheese and granulated sugar until well blended.
Mix in flour.

SHAPE dough into 1-inch balls; place on *ungreased* cookie sheets.

BAKE at 400°F for 10 to 13 minutes or until light golden brown and
set; cool on wire racks. Sprinkle with powdered sugar.

Makes about 6 dozen cookies

Variation: For holiday cookies tint dough with a few drops of food
coloring before shaping to add a festive touch.

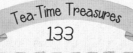

Chocolate Delights

Hershey's Best Brownies

1 cup (2 sticks) butter or margarine
2 cups sugar
2 teaspoons vanilla extract
4 eggs
¾ cup HERSHEY'S Cocoa or HERSHEY'S Dutch
    Processed Cocoa
1 cup all-purpose flour
½ teaspoon baking powder
¼ teaspoon salt
1 cup chopped nuts (optional)

1. Heat oven to 350°F. Grease 13×9×2-inch baking pan.

2. Place butter in large microwave-safe bowl. Microwave at HIGH (100% power) 2 to 2½ minutes or until melted. Stir in sugar and vanilla. Add eggs, one at a time, beating well with spoon after each addition. Add cocoa; beat until well blended. Add flour, baking powder and salt; beat well. Stir in nuts, if desired. Pour batter into prepared pan.

3. Bake 30 to 35 minutes or until brownies begin to pull away from sides of pan. Cool completely in pan on wire rack. Cut into bars. *Makes about 36 brownies*

Double Chocolate Cookies

2¼ cups all-purpose flour
1 teaspoon baking soda
1 teaspoon salt
1 cup (2 sticks) butter or margarine, softened
¾ cup granulated sugar
¾ cup packed brown sugar
1 teaspoon vanilla extract
2 large eggs
2 packets (1 ounce *each*) NESTLÉ® TOLL HOUSE®
  Choco-Bake® Unsweetened Chocolate Flavor
2 cups (12-ounce package) NESTLÉ® TOLL HOUSE®
  Semi-Sweet Chocolate Morsels
1 cup chopped walnuts (optional)

PREHEAT oven to 375°F.

COMBINE flour, baking soda and salt in small bowl. Beat butter, granulated sugar, brown sugar and vanilla extract in large mixer bowl until creamy. Beat in eggs and Choco Bake. Gradually beat in flour mixture. Stir in morsels and nuts. Drop by rounded tablespoon onto *ungreased* baking sheets.

BAKE for 8 to 10 minutes or until edges are set but centers are still slightly soft. Cool on baking sheets for 2 minutes; remove to wire racks to cool completely.   *Makes about 4 dozen cookies*

Chocolate Sugar Drops

½ cup (1 stick) butter, softened
½ cup vegetable oil
½ cup powdered sugar
½ cup granulated sugar
 1 egg
 2 cups all-purpose flour
¼ cup unsweetened cocoa powder
½ teaspoon baking soda
½ teaspoon cream of tartar
¼ teaspoon salt
 1 teaspoon vanilla
   Additional granulated sugar

1. Beat butter, oil, powdered sugar, ½ cup granulated sugar and egg in large bowl until light and fluffy. Combine flour, cocoa, baking soda, cream of tartar and salt in small bowl. Add to butter mixture with vanilla, stirring until dough is smooth. Cover; refrigerate 30 minutes or overnight, if desired.

2. Preheat oven to 350°F. Lightly grease cookie sheets or line with parchment paper. Shape dough into marble-sized balls. Place 2 inches apart on prepared cookie sheets. Flatten each cookie to about ⅓-inch thickness with bottom of greased glass dipped in additional granulated sugar.

3. Bake 10 minutes or until firm. *Do not overbake.* Remove to wire racks to cool.   *Makes about 5 dozen cookies*

Chocolate Crackles

⅓ cup **CRISCO® Oil***
1½ cups **granulated sugar**
1½ teaspoons **vanilla**
1 **egg**
2 **egg whites**
1⅔ cups **all-purpose flour**
½ cup **unsweetened cocoa powder**
1½ teaspoons **baking powder**
½ teaspoon **salt**
½ cup **confectioners' sugar**

Use your favorite Crisco Oil product.

1. Heat oven to 350°F. Place sheets of foil on countertop for cooling cookies.

2. Combine oil, granulated sugar and vanilla in large bowl. Beat at medium speed of electric mixer until blended. Add egg and egg whites. Beat until well blended. Stir in flour, cocoa, baking powder and salt with spoon.

3. Place confectioners' sugar in shallow dish or large plastic food storage bag.

4. Shape dough into 1-inch balls. Roll or shake in confectioners' sugar until coated. Place about 2 inches apart on *ungreased* baking sheet.

5. Bake at 350°F for 7 to 8 minutes or until almost no indentation remains when touched lightly. (Do not overbake.) Cool on baking sheet 2 minutes. Remove cookies to foil to cool completely.

Makes 4 dozen cookies

Chocolate Almond Cookies

1 cup (2 sticks) butter or margarine, softened
1 cup sugar
1 egg
½ teaspoon almond extract
½ teaspoon vanilla extract
2 cups all-purpose flour
½ cup HERSHEY'S Cocoa
¼ teaspoon baking powder
¼ teaspoon baking soda
⅛ teaspoon salt
1 cup HERSHEY'S MINI CHIPS™ Semi-Sweet
    Chocolate Chips
Additional sugar
Slivered blanched almonds

1. Beat butter and 1 cup sugar in large bowl until fluffy. Add egg, almond and vanilla extracts; beat well. Combine flour, cocoa, baking powder, baking soda and salt; gradually add to butter mixture, beating to form smooth dough. Stir in small chocolate chips. If necessary, refrigerate dough about 1 hour or until firm enough to handle.

2. Heat oven to 350°F. Shape dough into 1⅛-inch balls; roll in sugar. Place about 2 inches apart on *ungreased* cookie sheet. Place three slivered almonds on top of each ball; press slightly.

3. Bake 9 to 10 minutes or until set. Cool slightly. Remove from cookie sheet to wire rack. Cool completely.

Makes about 3½ dozen cookies

Hershey's Soft & Chewy Cookies

    1 cup (2 sticks) butter (no substitutes)
    ¾ cup packed light brown sugar
    ½ cup granulated sugar
    ¼ cup light corn syrup
    1 egg
    2 teaspoons vanilla extract
 2½ cups all-purpose flour
    1 teaspoon baking soda
    ¼ teaspoon salt
    1 package (10 or 12 ounces) HERSHEY'S Chips or
       Baking Bits (any flavor)

1. Heat oven to 350°F.

2. Beat butter, brown sugar and granulated sugar in large bowl until fluffy. Add corn syrup, egg and vanilla; beat well. Stir together flour, baking soda and salt; gradually add to butter mixture, beating until well blended. Stir in chips or bits. Drop by rounded teaspoons onto *ungreased* cookie sheet.

3. Bake 8 to 10 minutes or until lightly browned and almost set. Cool slightly; remove from cookie sheet to wire rack. Cool completely. Cookies will be softer the second day.

Makes about 3½ dozen cookies

Chocolate Chocolate Cookies: Decrease flour to 2¼ cups and add ¼ cup HERSHEY'S Cocoa or HERSHEY'S Dutch Processed Cocoa.

Cocoa Brownies

Prep Time: 20 minutes
Cook Time: 25 minutes
Total Time: 45 minutes

1¼ cups all-purpose flour
1 cup packed light brown sugar
¾ cup sugar
½ cup egg substitute
½ cup margarine or butter, melted
¼ cup unsweetened cocoa
1½ teaspoons vanilla extract
⅓ cup PLANTERS® Pecans, chopped
Powdered sugar

1. Mix flour, sugars, egg substitute, melted margarine and cocoa in large bowl until well blended. Stir in vanilla and pecans.

2. Spread in well-greased 13×9×2-inch baking pan. Bake in preheated 350°F oven for 25 minutes or until done. Cool in pan on wire rack. Dust with powdered sugar; cut into bars. *Makes 3 dozen*

Chewy Chocolate-Cinnamon Cookies

6 tablespoons butter or margarine, softened
⅔ cup packed light brown sugar
3 tablespoons plus ¼ cup granulated sugar, divided
1 egg
1 teaspoon baking soda
½ cup light corn syrup
1 teaspoon vanilla extract
1½ cups all-purpose flour
⅓ cup HERSHEY'S Cocoa
¼ to ½ teaspoon ground cinnamon

1. Heat oven to 350°F. Spray cookie sheet with nonstick cooking spray.

2. Beat butter until creamy. Add brown sugar and 3 tablespoons granulated sugar; beat until blended. Add egg, baking soda, corn syrup and vanilla; beat well.

3. Stir together flour and cocoa; beat into butter mixture. If batter becomes to stiff, use wooden spoon to stir in remaining flour. Cover; refrigerate about 30 minutes, if necessary, until batter is firm enough to shape. Shape dough into 1-inch balls. Combine ¼ cup granulated sugar and cinnamon; roll balls in mixture. Place balls 2 inches apart on prepared cookie sheet.

4. Bake 9 to 10 minutes or until cookies are set and tops are cracked. Cool slightly; remove from cookie sheet to wire rack. Cool completely. *Makes about 40 cookies*

Mini Morsel Meringue Cookies

Prep Time: 15 minutes
Cook Time: 20 minutes

  4 **large egg whites**
  ½ **teaspoon salt**
  ½ **teaspoon cream of tartar**
  1 **cup granulated sugar**
  2 **cups (12-ounce package) NESTLÉ® TOLL HOUSE®**
    Semi-Sweet Chocolate Mini Morsels

PREHEAT oven to 325°F. Grease baking sheets.

BEAT egg whites, salt and cream of tartar in small mixer bowl until soft peaks form. Gradually add sugar; beat until stiff peaks form. Gently fold morsels, ⅓ cup at a time. Drop by level tablespoons onto prepared baking sheets.

BAKE for 20 to 25 minutes or until meringues are dry and crisp. Cool on baking sheets for 2 minutes; remove to wire racks to cool completely. Store in airtight containers.

Makes about 5 dozen cookies

Chocolate Sandwich Cookies

Cookies
- 2 cups all-purpose flour
- ⅓ cup unsweetened cocoa powder
- 1 teaspoon baking soda
- ¼ teaspoon salt
- 6 tablespoons butter, softened
- 1 cup sugar
- 1 egg
- 1 cup milk

Filling
- ½ cup milk
- 2 tablespoons all-purpose flour
- ½ cup butter, softened
- ½ cup sugar
- 1 teaspoon vanilla

Preheat oven to 425°F. For cookies, stir together 2 cups flour, cocoa, baking soda and salt in medium bowl.

Beat 6 tablespoons butter and 1 cup sugar in large bowl until fluffy. Beat in egg. Add flour mixture and 1 cup milk alternately to butter mixture, beating after each addition. Drop dough by rounded teaspoonfuls onto greased cookie sheets. Bake about 7 minutes or until set. Remove to wire racks to cool.

For filling, stir together ½ cup milk and 2 tablespoons flour in small saucepan over low heat. Cook and stir until thick and bubbly; continue cooking 1 to 2 minutes more. Cool slightly. Beat ½ cup butter and ½ cup sugar in small bowl until fluffy. Add cooled flour mixture and vanilla. Beat until smooth. Spread filling on flat side of half the cooled cookies; top with remaining cookies.

Makes about 2½ dozen sandwich cookies

Favorite recipe from **Wisconsin Milk Marketing Board**

Hershey's Premium Double Chocolate Brownies

- ¾ cup **HERSHEY'S Cocoa**
- ½ **teaspoon baking soda**
- ⅔ **cup butter or margarine, melted and divided**
- ½ **cup boiling water**
- 2 **cups sugar**
- 2 **eggs**
- 1 **teaspoon vanilla extract**
- 1⅓ **cups all-purpose flour**
- ¼ **teaspoon salt**
- 2 **cups (12-ounce package) HERSHEY'S Semi-Sweet Chocolate Chips**
- ½ **cup coarsely chopped nuts (optional)**

1. Heat oven to 350°F. Grease 13×9×2-inch baking pan.

2. Stir together cocoa and baking soda in large bowl; stir in ⅓ cup butter. Add boiling water; stir until mixture thickens. Stir in sugar, eggs, remaining ⅓ cup butter and vanilla; stir until smooth. Gradually add flour and salt to cocoa mixture, beating until well blended. Stir in chocolate chips and nuts, if desired; pour batter into prepared pan.

3. Bake 35 to 40 minutes or until brownies begin to pull away from sides of pan. Cool completely in pan on wire rack. Cut into bars.

Makes about 36 brownies

Chocolate Covered Cherry Cookies

   1 cup sugar
   ½ cup butter, softened
   1 egg
 1½ teaspoons vanilla
 1½ cups all-purpose flour
   ¼ cup unsweetened cocoa powder
   ¼ teaspoon baking powder
   ¼ teaspoon baking soda
   ¼ teaspoon salt
  42 maraschino cherries, drained, reserving 4 to 5 teaspoons
      juice
   1 (6-ounce) package semi-sweet chocolate pieces
   ½ cup sweetened condensed milk

Beat sugar and butter in large bowl until light and fluffy. Blend in egg
and vanilla. Combine flour, cocoa, baking powder, baking soda and
salt in small bowl. Add to sugar mixture; mix well. Shape dough into
1-inch balls; place on *ungreased* cookie sheets. Indent centers; fill each
with 1 cherry. Combine chocolate pieces and sweetened condensed
milk in small saucepan; stir over low heat until smooth. Blend in
enough cherry juice to reach spreading consistency. Drop 1 teaspoon
chocolate mixture over each cherry, spreading to cover cherry. Bake in
preheated 350°F oven 12 minutes or until set. *Makes 3½ dozen*

Favorite recipe from **Wisconsin Milk Marketing Board**

Sour Cream Brownies

Brownies
- 1 cup water
- 1 cup butter
- 3 tablespoons unsweetened cocoa powder
- 2 cups all-purpose flour
- 2 cups granulated sugar
- 1 teaspoon baking soda
- ½ teaspoon salt
- 1 (8-ounce) container dairy sour cream
- 2 eggs

Frosting
- 4 cups sifted powdered sugar
- 3 tablespoons unsweetened cocoa powder
- ½ cup butter, softened
- 6 tablespoons milk
- 1 cup chopped nuts

For brownies, preheat oven to 350°F. Grease 15×10×1-inch baking pan; set aside. Combine water, butter and cocoa in medium saucepan. Cook, stirring constantly, until mixture comes to a boil. Remove from heat; set aside. Combine flour, granulated sugar, baking soda and salt in medium bowl; set aside.

Beat sour cream and eggs at medium speed of electric mixer. Gradually add hot cocoa mixture, beating well. Blend in flour mixture; beat until smooth. Pour batter into prepared pan. Bake 25 to 30 minutes or until brownie springs back when lightly touched. Cool completely in pan on wire rack.

For frosting, combine powdered sugar and cocoa in large bowl; set aside. Beat butter in medium bowl at medium speed of electric mixer until creamy. Add powdered sugar mixture alternately with milk, beating well after each addition. Spread over cooled brownies. Sprinkle nuts over frosting. *Makes about 40 brownies*

Favorite recipe from **Wisconsin Milk Marketing Board**

Best Brownies

½ cup (1 stick) butter or margarine, melted
1 cup sugar
1 teaspoon vanilla extract
2 eggs
½ cup all-purpose flour
⅓ cup HERSHEY'S Cocoa
¼ teaspoon baking powder
¼ teaspoon salt
½ cup chopped nuts (optional)
Creamy Brownie Frosting (recipe follows)

1. Heat oven to 350°F. Grease 9-inch square baking pan.

2. Stir together butter, sugar and vanilla in large bowl. Add eggs; beat well with spoon. Combine flour, cocoa, baking powder and salt; gradually add to butter mixture, beating until well blended. Stir in nuts. Spread into prepared pan.

3. Bake 20 to 25 minutes or until brownies begin to pull away from sides of pan. Cool; frost with Creamy Brownie Frosting. Cut into squares. *Makes about 16 brownies*

Creamy Brownie Frosting

3 tablespoons butter or margarine, softened
3 tablespoons HERSHEY'S Cocoa
1 tablespoon light corn syrup or honey
½ teaspoon vanilla extract
1 cup powdered sugar
1 to 2 tablespoons milk

Beat butter, cocoa, corn syrup and vanilla in small bowl. Add powdered sugar and milk; beat to spreading consistency.
Makes about 1 cup frosting

Mocha Crinkles

1⅓ cups packed light brown sugar
½ cup vegetable oil
¼ cup low-fat sour cream
1 egg
1 teaspoon vanilla
1¾ cups all-purpose flour
¾ cup unsweetened cocoa powder
2 teaspoons instant espresso or coffee granules
1 teaspoon baking soda
¼ teaspoon salt
⅛ teaspoon black pepper
½ cup powdered sugar

1. Beat brown sugar and oil in medium bowl with electric mixer. Mix in sour cream, egg and vanilla. Set aside.

2. Mix flour, cocoa, espresso, baking soda, salt and pepper in another medium bowl.

3. Add flour mixture to brown sugar mixture; mix well. Cover; refrigerate dough 3 to 4 hours or until firm.

4. Preheat oven to 350°F. Pour powdered sugar into shallow bowl. Set aside. Cut dough into 1-inch pieces; roll into balls. Roll balls in powdered sugar.

5. Bake on *ungreased* cookie sheets 10 to 12 minutes or until tops of cookies are firm to touch. *Do not overbake.* Cool on wire racks.

Makes 72 cookies

German Chocolate Brownie Cookies

Cookies
- 1½ cups firmly packed light brown sugar
- ⅔ CRISCO® Stick or ⅔ cup CRISCO® all-vegetable shortening
- 1 tablespoon water
- 1 teaspoon vanilla
- 2 eggs
- 1½ cups all-purpose flour
- ⅓ cup unsweetened cocoa powder
- ½ teaspoon salt
- ¼ teaspoon baking soda
- 2 cups (12 ounces) semisweet chocolate chips

Topping
- ½ cup evaporated milk
- ½ cup granulated sugar
- ¼ Butter Flavor CRISCO® Stick or ¼ cup Butter Flavor CRISCO® all-vegetable shortening
- 2 egg yolks, lightly beaten
- ½ teaspoon vanilla
- ½ cup chopped pecans
- ½ cup flaked coconut

1. Heat oven to 375°F. Place sheets of foil on countertop for cooling cookies.

2. For cookies, place brown sugar, shortening, water and vanilla in large bowl. Beat at medium speed of electric mixer until well blended. Add eggs; beat well.

3. Combine flour, cocoa, salt and baking soda. Add to shortening mixture; beat at low speed just until blended. Stir in chocolate chips.

4. Drop dough by rounded measuring tablespoonfuls 2 inches apart onto *ungreased* baking sheet.

5. Bake one baking sheet at a time at 375°F for 7 to 9 minutes or until cookies are set. *Do not overbake.* Cool 2 minutes on baking sheet. Remove cookies to foil to cool completely.

Chocolate Delights
150

6. For topping, combine evaporated milk, granulated sugar, shortening and egg yolks in medium saucepan. Stir over medium heat until thickened. Remove from heat. Stir in vanilla, pecans and coconut. Cool completely. Frost cookies. *Makes about 3 dozen cookies*

Note: Crisco® Stick or Crisco all-vegetable shortening can be substituted for Butter Flavor Crisco Stick or Butter Flavor Crisco all-vegetable shortening.

Hershey's Doubly Chocolate Cookies

  2 cups all-purpose flour
  ⅔ cup HERSHEY'S Cocoa
  ¾ teaspoon baking soda
  ¼ teaspoon salt
  1 cup (2 sticks) butter or margarine, softened
1½ cups sugar
  2 eggs
  2 teaspoons vanilla extract
  2 cups (12-ounce package) HERSHEY'S Semi-Sweet Chocolate Chips or 2 cups (11½-ounce package) HERSHEY'S Milk Chocolate Chips
  ½ cup coarsely chopped nuts (optional)

1. Heat oven to 350°F.

2. Stir together flour, cocoa, baking soda and salt. Beat butter, sugar, eggs and vanilla in large bowl until fluffy. Gradually add flour mixture, beating well. Stir in choclate chips and nuts, if desired. Drop by rounded teaspoons onto *ungreased* cookie sheet.

3. Bake 8 to 10 minutes or just until set. Cool slightly; remove from cookie sheet to wire rack. Cool completely.
Makes about 4½ dozen cookies

Chocolate Nut Slices

¾ **Butter Flavor CRISCO® Stick or ¾ cup Butter Flavor CRISCO® all-vegetable shortening**
½ **cup granulated sugar**
⅓ **cup firmly packed brown sugar**
2 **tablespoons milk**
1½ **teaspoons vanilla**
1 **egg**
1¼ **cups all-purpose flour**
⅓ **cup unsweetened cocoa powder**
½ **teaspoon baking soda**
½ **teaspoon salt**
¾ **cup coarsely chopped pecans**
½ **cup semi-sweet chocolate chips**

Drizzle
½ **teaspoon Butter Flavor CRISCO® Stick or ½ teaspoon Butter Flavor CRISCO® all-vegetable shortening**
½ **cup white melting chocolate, cut into small pieces**
Chopped pecans (optional)

1. Heat oven to 350°F. Place sheets of foil on countertop for cooling cookies.

2. For cookies, combine shortening, granulated sugar, brown sugar, milk and vanilla in large bowl. Beat at medium speed of electric mixer until well blended. Beat in egg.

3. Combine flour, cocoa, baking soda and salt. Mix into creamed mixture at low speed until blended. Stir in nuts and chocolate chips.

4. Divide dough into 4 equal portions. Form each into 1×8-inch roll. Make dough rolls on waxed paper. Pick up ends of waxed paper and roll dough back and forth to get a nicely shaped roll. Place 3 inches apart on *ungreased* baking sheet.

5. Bake at 350°F for 10 minutes, or until set. *Do not overbake.* Cool 2 minutes on baking sheet. Remove cookies to foil to cool completely.

6. For drizzle, combine shortening and white chocolate in microwave-safe cup. Microwave at MEDIUM (50% power). Stir after 1 minute. Repeat until smooth (or melt on rangetop in small saucepan on very low heat). Drizzle back and forth over cooled cookie. Sprinkle with nuts before chocolate hardens, if desired.

7. Cut diagonally into 1-inch slices.   *Makes about 3 dozen cookies*

Fudge Kisses

  1 cup (6 ounces) semisweet chocolate chips
  2 egg whites
  Dash salt
½ teaspoon cider vinegar
½ teaspoon vanilla
½ cup sugar
½ cup flaked coconut
¼ cup chopped walnuts or pecans

1. Preheat oven to 350°F. Line cookie sheets with parchment paper or lightly grease and sprinkle with flour.

2. Melt chocolate chips in top of double boiler over hot, not boiling, water. Remove from heat; cool. In large clean, dry bowl, beat egg whites with salt until frothy. Beat in vinegar and vanilla. Beat in sugar, one tablespoon at a time, until mixture becomes stiff and glossy. Gently fold in coconut, nuts and melted chocolate until mixture is marbled.

3. Drop mixture by rounded teaspoonfuls 2 inches apart onto prepared cookie sheets. Bake 12 to 15 minutes or until dry on top. Cool completely on cookie sheets. Store in airtight containers.

Makes 3 dozen cookies

Cocoa Snickerdoodles

- **1 cup (2 sticks) butter, softened**
- **¾ cup packed brown sugar**
- **¾ cup plus 2 tablespoons granulated sugar, divided**
- **2 eggs**
- **2 cups uncooked old-fashioned oats**
- **1½ cups all-purpose flour**
- **¼ cup plus 2 tablespoons unsweetened cocoa powder, divided**
- **1 teaspoon baking soda**
- **2 tablespoons ground cinnamon**

1. Preheat oven to 375°F. Lightly grease cookie sheets or line with parchment paper.

2. Beat butter, brown sugar and ¾ cup granulated sugar in large bowl until light and fluffy. Add eggs; mix well. Combine oats, flour, ¼ cup cocoa and baking soda in medium bowl. Stir into butter mixture until blended.

3. Mix remaining 2 tablespoons granulated sugar, remaining 2 tablespoons cocoa and cinnamon in small bowl. Drop dough by rounded teaspoonfuls into cinnamon mixture; toss to coat. Place 2 inches apart on prepared cookie sheets.

4. Bake 8 to 10 minutes or until firm in center. *Do not overbake.* Remove to wire racks to cool. *Makes about 4½ dozen cookies*

Deep Dark Chocolate Cookies

  ¾ **cup (1½ sticks) butter or margarine, softened**
  ¾ **cup granulated sugar**
  ½ **cup packed light brown sugar**
   1 **teaspoon vanilla extract**
   2 **eggs**
1¾ **cups all-purpose flour**
  ½ **cup HERSHEY₌S Cocoa**
  ¾ **teaspoon baking soda**
  ½ **teaspoon baking powder**
  ¼ **teaspoon salt**
   1 **cup HERSHEY₌S Semi-Sweet Chocolate Chips**
  ½ **cup chopped nuts**

1. Heat oven to 375°F.

2. Beat butter, granulated sugar, brown sugar and vanilla in large bowl on medium speed of mixer 2 minutes or until fluffy. Add eggs; beat well. Stir together flour, cocoa, baking soda, baking powder and salt; gradually add to butter mixture, beating just until blended. Stir in chocolate chips and nuts. Drop dough by heaping teaspoonfuls onto *ungreased* cookie sheet.

3. Bake 7 minutes or until set. Cool 1 minute; remove from cookie sheet to wire rack. Cool completely.   *Makes about 4 dozen cookies*

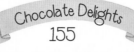

Cracked Chocolate Cookies

1½ **cups firmly packed light brown sugar**
⅔ **CRISCO® Stick or ⅔ cup CRISCO® all-vegetable**
    shortening
1 **tablespoon water**
1 **teaspoon vanilla**
2 **eggs**
1½ **cups all-purpose flour**
⅓ **cup unsweetened cocoa powder**
½ **teaspoon salt**
¼ **teaspoon baking soda**
2 **cups (12 ounces) miniature semisweet chocolate chips**
1 **cup confectioners' sugar**

1. Heat oven to 375°F. Place sheets of foil on countertop for cooling cookies.

2. Place brown sugar, shortening, water and vanilla in large bowl. Beat at medium speed of electric mixer until well blended. Add eggs; beat well.

3. Combine flour, cocoa, salt and baking soda. Add to shortening mixture; beat at low speed just until blended. Stir in miniature chocolate chips.

4. Shape dough into 1¼-inch balls. Roll in confectioners' sugar. Place 2 inches apart on *ungreased* baking sheets.

5. Bake one baking sheet at a time at 375°F for 7 to 9 minutes or until cookies are set. *Do not overbake.* Cool 2 minutes on baking sheet. Remove cookies to foil to cool completely.

Makes about 4 dozen cookies

Date Fudge Cookies

- **1 cup (6 ounces) semisweet chocolate chips**
- **½ cup (1 stick) butter, softened**
- **1 cup granulated sugar**
- **2 eggs**
- **1½ cups all-purpose flour**
- **Dash salt**
- **1 package (8 ounces) chopped pitted dates**
- **½ cup coarsely chopped pecans or walnuts**
- **Brown Sugar Icing (recipe follows)**

1. Preheat oven to 375°F. Lightly grease cookie sheets or line with parchment paper. Melt chocolate chips in top of double boiler over hot, not boiling, water. Remove from heat; cool. Cream butter, granulated sugar and eggs in large bowl until smooth. Beat in melted chocolate. Gradually add flour and salt, mixing until smooth. Stir in dates and pecans.

2. Drop dough by rounded teaspoonfuls 2 inches apart onto prepared cookie sheets. Bake 10 to 12 minutes or until slightly firm. Cool 5 minutes on cookie sheets, then remove to wire racks. While cookies bake, prepare Brown Sugar Icing. Spread over cookies while still warm. Cool until icing is set. *Makes about 5 dozen cookies*

Brown Sugar Icing

- **½ cup packed dark brown sugar**
- **¼ cup water**
- **2 squares (1 ounce each) unsweetened chocolate**
- **2 cups powdered sugar**
- **¼ cup (½ stick) butter or margarine**
- **1 teaspoon vanilla**

Combine brown sugar, water and chocolate in small heavy saucepan. Stir over medium heat until chocolate is melted and mixture boils. Boil 1 minute. Remove from heat; beat in powdered sugar, butter and vanilla. Continue beating until mixture has cooled slightly and thickened. Spread over cookies while icing is still warm.

Chocolate-Cherry Slice 'n' Bake Cookies

¾ cup (1½ sticks) **butter or margarine, softened**
1 **cup sugar**
1 **egg**
1½ **teaspoons vanilla extract**
2¼ **cups all-purpose flour**
2 **teaspoons baking powder**
½ **teaspoon salt**
¼ **cup finely chopped maraschino cherries**
½ **teaspoon almond extract**
   Red food color
⅓ **cup HERSHEY'S Cocoa**
¼ **teaspoon baking soda**
4 **teaspoons water**
   Cocoa Almond Glaze (recipe page 159)

1. Beat butter, sugar, egg and vanilla in large bowl until fluffy. Stir together flour, baking powder and salt; gradually add to butter mixture, beating until mixture forms a smooth dough. Remove 1¼ cups dough to medium bowl; blend in cherries, almond extract and about 6 drops food color.

2. Stir together cocoa and baking soda. Add with water to remaining dough; blend until smooth. Divide chocolate dough in half; roll each half between two sheets of wax paper, forming 12×4½-inch rectangle. Remove top sheet of wax paper. Divide cherry mixture in half; with floured hands, shape each half into 12-inch roll. Place one roll in center of each rectangle; wrap chocolate dough around roll, forming one large roll. Wrap in plastic wrap. Refrigerate about 6 hours or until firm.

3. Heat oven to 350°F.

4. Cut rolls into ¼-inch-thick slices; place on *ungreased* cookie sheet. Bake 7 minutes or until set. Cool 1 minute; remove from cookie sheet to wire rack. Cool completely. Prepare Cocoa Almond Glaze; decorate cookies. *Makes about 7½ dozen cookies*

Cocoa Almond Glaze

- **2 tablespoons butter or margarine**
- **2 tablespoons HERSHEY'S Cocoa**
- **2 tablespoons water**
- **1 cup powdered sugar**
- **⅛ teaspoon almond extract**

Melt butter in small saucepan over low heat. Add cocoa and water; stir constantly until mixture thickens. *Do not boil.* Remove from heat. Add sugar and almond extract, beating until smooth and of desired consistency. Add additional water, ½ teaspoon at a time, if needed.

Makes about ¾ cup glaze

Chocolate Walnut Meringues

- **3 egg whites**
- **Pinch of salt**
- **¾ cup sugar**
- **½ cup good-quality Dutch-processed cocoa**
- **⅓ cup finely chopped California walnuts**

Preheat oven to 350°F. Place egg whites and salt in large mixing bowl. Beat with electric mixer or wire whisk until soft peaks form. Gradually add sugar, beating until stiff peaks form. Sift cocoa over peaks and fold into egg white mixture with walnuts. Spoon mounds about 1 inch in diameter and about 1 inch apart onto parchment-lined baking sheets. Bake 20 minutes or until dry to the touch. Let cool completely before removing from baking sheets. Store in airtight container.

Makes 48 cookies

Favorite recipe from **Walnut Marketing Board**

Chocolate Sugar Cookies

Prep Time: 20 minutes plus refrigerating
Bake Time: 10 minutes

- **2 cups flour**
- **1 teaspoon baking soda**
- **¼ teaspoon salt**
- **3 squares BAKER'S® Unsweetened Baking Chocolate**
- **1 cup (2 sticks) butter or margarine**
- **1 cup sugar**
- **1 egg**
- **1 teaspoon vanilla**
- **Additional sugar**

HEAT oven to 375°F. Mix flour, baking soda and salt in medium bowl.

MICROWAVE chocolate and butter in large microwavable bowl on HIGH 2 minutes or until butter is melted. Stir until chocolate is completely melted.

STIR 1 cup sugar into melted chocolate mixture until well blended. Mix in egg and vanilla until completely blended. Stir in flour mixture until well blended. Refrigerate dough about 15 minutes or until easy to handle.

SHAPE dough into 1-inch balls; roll in additional sugar. Place on *ungreased* cookie sheets.

BAKE 8 to 10 minutes or until set. (If flatter, crisper cookies are desired, flatten with bottom of glass before baking.) Remove from cookie sheets. Cool on wire racks. Store in tightly covered container.

Makes about 3½ dozen cookies

Jam-Filled Chocolate Sugar Cookies: **Prepare Baker's® Chocolate Sugar Cookie dough as directed. Roll in finely chopped nuts in place of sugar. Make indentation in each ball; fill center with your favorite jam. Bake as directed.**

Double Chocolate Oat Cookies

1 package (12 ounces) semisweet chocolate pieces, divided (about 2 cups)
½ cup (1 stick) margarine or butter, softened
½ cup granulated sugar
1 egg
¼ teaspoon vanilla
¾ cup all-purpose flour
¾ cup QUAKER® Oats (quick or old fashioned, uncooked)
1 teaspoon baking powder
¼ teaspoon baking soda
¼ teaspoon salt (optional)

Preheat oven to 375°F. Melt 1 cup chocolate pieces in small saucepan; set aside. Beat margarine and sugar until fluffy; add melted chocolate, egg and vanilla. Add combined flour, oats, baking powder, baking soda and salt; mix well. Stir in remaining chocolate pieces. Drop by rounded tablespoonfuls onto *ungreased* cookie sheets. Bake 8 to 10 minutes. Cool 1 minute on cookie sheets; remove to wire rack.

Makes about 3 dozen cookies

French Vanilla

Double Chocolate Drops

1⅓ **Butter Flavor CRISCO® Stick or 1⅓ cup Butter Flavor CRISCO® all-vegetable shortening**
  1 **cup granulated sugar**
  ⅔ **cup firmly packed brown sugar**
  3 **tablespoons milk**
  1 **tablespoon vanilla**
  2 **eggs**
2¼ **cups all-purpose flour**
  ⅔ **cup unsweetened cocoa powder**
  1 **teaspoon baking soda**
  1 **teaspoon salt**
1½ **cups coarsely chopped walnuts or pecans**
  1 **cup semi-sweet chocolate chips**

1. Heat oven to 350°F. Place sheets of foil on countertop for cooling cookies.

2. Combine shortening, granulated sugar, brown sugar, milk and vanilla in large bowl. Beat at medium speed of electric mixer until well blended. Add eggs one at a time. Beat well after each addition.

3. Combine flour, cocoa, baking soda and salt. Mix into creamed mixture at low speed until just blended. Stir in nuts and chips.

4. Drop 2 level tablespoonfuls of dough into a mound 3 inches apart onto *ungreased* baking sheet. Repeat for each cookie.

5. Bake at 350°F for 9 to 11 minutes or until set. *Do not overbake.* Cool 2 minutes on baking sheet. Remove cookies to foil to cool completely.

Makes about 2 dozen cookies

Cook's Tip: For smaller cookies, drop 1 rounded tablespoonful of dough for each cookie. Place 2 inches apart on baking sheet. Bake at 350°F for 7 to 9 minutes or until set. Cool 2 minutes on baking sheet. Remove to cooling rack.

Chocolate Macaroons

  1 **can (8 ounces) almond paste**
  ½ **cup powdered sugar**
  2 **egg whites**
12 **ounces semisweet baking chocolate or chips, melted**
  2 **tablespoons all-purpose flour**
     Powdered sugar (optional)

1. Preheat oven to 300°F. Line cookie sheets with parchment paper; set aside.

2. Beat almond paste, ½ cup powdered sugar and egg whites in large bowl with electric mixer at medium speed for 1 minute, scraping down side of bowl once. Beat in chocolate until well combined. Beat in flour at low speed, scraping down side of bowl once.

3. Spoon dough into pastry bag fitted with rosette tip. Pipe 1½-inch spirals 1 inch apart on prepared cookie sheets. Pipe all cookies at once; dough will get stiff upon standing.

4. Bake 20 minutes or until set. Carefully transfer parchment paper with cookies to countertop. Let cookies cool completely.

5. Peel cookies off parchment paper. Sprinkle powdered sugar over cookies, if desired. *Makes about 3 dozen cookies*

Classic Cutouts

Sugar Cookies

- **1 cup sugar**
- **1 cup (2 sticks) butter, softened**
- **2 eggs**
- **½ teaspoon lemon extract**
- **½ teaspoon vanilla extract**
- **3 cups all-purpose flour**
- **1 teaspoon baking powder**
- **¼ teaspoon salt**
- **Colored sugar**

1. Beat sugar and butter in large bowl with electric mixer at medium speed until light and fluffy. Beat in eggs and extracts until well blended (mixture will look grainy). Beat in 1 cup flour, baking powder and salt until well blended. Gradually add remaining 2 cups flour. Beat at low speed until soft dough forms. Divide dough into 3 discs. Wrap discs in plastic wrap; refrigerate 2 hours or until dough is firm.

2. Preheat oven to 375°F. Working with 1 disc at a time, unwrap dough and place on lightly floured surface. Roll out dough with lightly floured rolling pin to ⅛-inch thickness. Cut dough with lightly floured cookie cutters. Sprinkle with colored sugar. Place cutouts 1 inch apart on *ungreased* cookie sheets. Gently press dough trimmings together; reroll and cut out more cookies. (If dough is sticky, pat into disc; wrap in plastic wrap and refrigerate until firm before rerolling.)

3. Bake 7 to 9 minutes or until cookies are set. Remove cookies to cool on wire rack. Store loosely covered at room temperature up to 1 week.   *Makes about 3 dozen cookies*

Lemony Butter Cookies

½ cup (1 stick) butter, softened
½ cup sugar
1 egg
1½ cups all-purpose flour
2 tablespoons fresh lemon juice
1 teaspoon grated lemon peel
½ teaspoon baking powder
⅛ teaspoon salt
Additional sugar

1. Beat butter and sugar in large bowl with electric mixer at medium speed until creamy. Beat in egg until light and fluffy. Mix in flour, lemon juice and peel, baking powder and salt. Cover; refrigerate about 2 hours or until firm.

2. Preheat oven to 350°F. Roll out dough, small portion at a time, on well-floured surface to ¼-inch thickness. (Keep remaining dough in refrigerator.) Cut with 3-inch round or fluted cookie cutter. Transfer to *ungreased* cookie sheets. Sprinkle with sugar.

3. Bake 8 to 10 minutes or until edges are lightly browned. Cool 1 minute on cookie sheets. Remove to wire racks; cool completely. Store in airtight container.   *Makes about 2½ dozen cookies*

Classic Cutouts

Moravian Spice Crisps

⅓ cup shortening
⅓ cup packed brown sugar
¼ cup dark molasses
¼ cup dark corn syrup
1¾ to 2 cups all-purpose flour
2 teaspoons ground ginger
1¼ teaspoons baking soda
1 teaspoon ground cinnamon
½ teaspoon ground cloves
Powdered sugar

1. Melt shortening in small saucepan over low heat. Remove from heat; stir in brown sugar, molasses and corn syrup. Set aside; cool.

2. Place 1½ cups flour, ginger, baking soda, cinnamon and cloves in large bowl; stir to combine. Beat in shortening mixture. Gradually beat in remaining ¼ cup flour to form stiff dough.

3. Knead dough on lightly floured surface, adding more flour if too sticky. Form dough into 2 discs; wrap in plastic wrap and refrigerate 30 minutes or until firm.

4. Preheat oven to 350°F. Grease cookie sheets; set aside. Working with 1 disc at a time, roll out dough on lightly floured surface to 1/16-inch thickness.

5. Cut dough with floured 2⅜-inch scalloped cookie cutter. (If dough becomes too soft, refrigerate several minutes before continuing.) Gently press dough trimmings together; reroll and cut out more cookies. Place cutouts ½ inch apart on prepared cookie sheets.

6. Bake 8 minutes or until firm and lightly browned. Remove cookies to wire racks; cool completely.

7. To make designs on top of cookies, place small strips of cardboard or parchment paper cutouts over cookies; dust with sifted powdered sugar. Carefully remove cardboard.   *Makes about 6 dozen cookies*

Ultimate Sugar Cookies

1¼ cups granulated sugar
1 Butter Flavor CRISCO® Stick or 1 cup Butter Flavor
    CRISCO® all-vegetable shortening
2 eggs
¼ cup light corn syrup or regular pancake syrup
1 tablespoon vanilla
3 cups all-purpose flour plus 4 tablespoons, divided
¾ teaspoon baking powder
½ teaspoon baking soda
½ teaspoon salt
    Decorations of your choice: granulated sugar, colored
        sugar crystals, frosting, decors, candies, chips, nuts,
        raisins, decorating gel

1. Combine sugar and shortening in large bowl. Beat at medium speed of electric mixer until well blended. Add eggs, syrup and vanilla. Beat until well blended and fluffy.

2. Combine 3 cups flour, baking powder, baking soda and salt. Add gradually to creamed mixture at low speed. Mix until well blended. Divide dough into 4 quarters. For well-defined cookie edges, or if dough is too sticky or too soft to roll, do the following. Wrap each quarter of dough with plastic wrap. Refrigerate 1 hour. Keep dough balls refrigerated until ready to roll.

3. Heat oven to 375°F. Place sheets of foil on countertop for cooling cookies.

4. Spread 1 tablespoon flour on large sheet of waxed paper. Place ¼ of dough on floured paper. Flatten slightly with hands. Turn dough over and cover with another large sheet of waxed paper. Roll dough to ¼-inch thickness. Remove top sheet of waxed paper.

5. Cut out cookies with floured cutter. Transfer to *ungreased* baking sheet with large pancake turner. Place 2 inches apart. Roll out remaining dough. Sprinkle with granulated sugar, colored sugar crystals, decors or leave plain to frost or decorate when cooled.

6. Bake one baking sheet at a time at 375°F for 5 to 9 minutes, depending on the size of your cookies (bake smaller, thinner cookies closer to 5 minutes: larger cookies closer to 9 minutes). *Do not overbake.* Cool 2 minutes on baking sheet. Remove cookies to foil to cool completely, then frost if desired.

Makes about 3 to 4 dozen cookies

Gingerbread Cookies

½ **cup shortening**
⅓ **cup packed light brown sugar**
¼ **cup dark molasses**
1 **egg white**
½ **teaspoon vanilla**
1½ **cups all-purpose flour**
1 **teaspoon ground cinnamon**
½ **teaspoon baking soda**
½ **teaspoon salt**
½ **teaspoon ground ginger**
¼ **teaspoon baking powder**

1. Beat shortening, brown sugar, molasses, egg white and vanilla in large bowl at high speed of electric mixer until smooth. Combine flour, cinnamon, baking soda, salt, ginger and baking powder in small bowl. Add to shortening mixture; mix well. Cover; refrigerate until firm, about 8 hours or overnight.

2. Preheat oven to 350°F. Grease cookie sheets.

3. Roll dough on lightly floured surface to ⅛-inch thickness. Cut into desired shapes with cookie cutters. Place on prepared cookie sheets.

4. Bake 6 to 8 minutes or until edges begin to brown. Remove to wire racks; cool completely.

Makes about 2½ dozen cookies

Frosted Sugar Cookies

½ **cup (1 stick) plus 2 tablespoons margarine, softened**
1 **cup sugar**
2 **egg whites**
1 **teaspoon vanilla**
2 **cups all-purpose flour**
1 **teaspoon baking powder**
½ **teaspoon salt**
   Vanilla Frosting (recipe page 171)
   Ground nutmeg or cinnamon

1. Preheat oven to 375°F. Spray cookie sheets with nonstick cooking spray.

2. Beat margarine and sugar in large bowl with electric mixer at medium speed until fluffy. Beat in egg whites and vanilla.

3. Combine flour, baking powder and salt in medium bowl. Add flour mixture to margarine mixture; mix well. Refrigerate 3 to 4 hours.

4. Roll out dough on generously floured surface to ¼-inch thickness (dough will be soft). Cut decorative shapes out of dough with 2-inch cookie cutters and place on prepared cookie sheets.

5. Bake 8 to 10 minutes or until cookies turn golden brown. Remove from cookie sheets to wire racks; cool completely. Meanwhile, prepare Vanilla Frosting.

6. Frost cookies; sprinkle with nutmeg or cinnamon.

Makes 7 dozen cookies

Cook·s Tips: To avoid having the cookie dough stick to the cookie cutter, dip the cutter in flour before each use. To get the most cookies out of the dough, cut cookies as close together as possible. Press dough scraps together, being careful not to overhandle them. Then, reroll dough on floured surface and continue to cut more cookies.

Vanilla Frosting

2 cups powdered sugar
2 to 3 tablespoons fat-free (skim) milk, divided
1 teaspoon vanilla

Mix powdered sugar, 2 tablespoons milk and vanilla in medium bowl with fork. Add additional 1 tablespoon milk until desired spreading consistency is reached.   *Makes about ½ cup frosting*

Old-Fashioned Molasses Cookies

4 cups sifted all-purpose flour
2 teaspoons ARM & HAMMER® Baking Soda
2 teaspoons ground ginger
1 teaspoon ground cinnamon
⅛ teaspoon salt
1½ cups molasses
½ cup butter-flavored shortening
¼ cup butter or margarine, melted
⅓ cup boiling water
   Sugar

In medium bowl, combine flour, baking soda, spices and salt. In large bowl, mix molasses, shortening, butter and water. Add dry ingredients to molasses mixture; blend well. Cover; refrigerate until firm, about 2 hours. Roll out dough ¼ inch thick on well-floured surface. Cut out with 3½-inch cookie cutters; sprinkle with sugar. Place 2 inches apart on *ungreased* cookie sheets. Bake in preheated 375°F oven about 12 minutes. Remove to wire racks to cool.
                                   Makes about 3 dozen cookies

Frosted Butter Cookies

Cookies
- 1½ cups (3 sticks) butter, softened
- ¾ cup granulated sugar
- 3 egg yolks
- 3 cups all-purpose flour
- 1 teaspoon baking powder
- 2 tablespoons orange juice
- 1 teaspoon vanilla

Frosting
- 4 cups powdered sugar
- ½ cup (1 stick) butter, softened
- 3 to 4 tablespoons milk
- 2 teaspoons vanilla
- Food coloring (optional)
- Colored sugars, flaked coconut and cinnamon candies for decoration

1. For cookies, cream butter and granulated sugar, in large bowl. Add egg yolks; beat until light and fluffy. Add flour, baking powder, orange juice and vanilla; beat until well mixed. Cover; refrigerate 2 to 3 hours or until firm.

2. Preheat oven to 350°F. Roll out dough, half at a time, to ¼-inch thickness on well-floured surface. Cut out with your favorite cookie cutters. Place 1 inch apart on *ungreased* cookie sheets. Bake 6 to 10 minutes or until edges are golden brown. Remove to wire racks to cool completely.

3. For frosting, beat powdered sugar, butter, milk and vanilla in bowl until fluffy. If desired, divide frosting into small bowls and tint with food coloring. Frost cookies; decorate as desired.

Makes about 3 dozen cookies

Cinnamon Stars

2 tablespoons sugar
¾ teaspoon ground cinnamon
¾ cup butter or margarine, softened
2 egg yolks
1 teaspoon vanilla extract
1 package DUNCAN HINES® Moist Deluxe® French Vanilla Cake Mix

1. Preheat oven to 375°F. Combine sugar and cinnamon in small bowl. Set aside.

2. Combine butter, egg yolks and vanilla extract in large bowl. Blend in cake mix gradually. Roll to ⅛-inch thickness on lightly floured surface. Cut with 2½-inch star cookie cutter. Place 2 inches apart on *ungreased* baking sheet.

3. Sprinkle cookies with cinnamon-sugar mixture. Bake at 375°F for 6 to 8 minutes or until edges are light golden brown. Cool 1 minute on baking sheet. Remove to cooling rack. Cool completely. Store in airtight container.   *Makes 3 to 3½ dozen cookies*

Cook's Tip: You can use your favorite cookie cutter in place of the star cookie cutter.

Chocolate and Peanut Butter Hearts

Chocolate Cookie Dough (recipe page 175)
½ **cup shortening**
½ **cup creamy peanut butter**
1 **cup sugar**
1 **egg**
3 **tablespoons milk**
1 **teaspoon vanilla**
2 **cups all-purpose flour**
1 **teaspoon baking powder**
¼ **teaspoon salt**

1. Prepare and chill Chocolate Cookie Dough as directed.

2. Beat shortening, peanut butter and sugar until fluffy. Add egg, milk and vanilla; mix well. Combine flour, baking powder and salt. Beat flour mixture into peanut butter mixture until well blended. Shape dough into disc. Wrap in plastic wrap; refrigerate 1 to 2 hours or until firm.

3. Preheat oven to 350°F. Grease cookie sheets. Roll peanut butter dough on floured waxed paper to ⅛-inch thickness. Cut dough using 3-inch heart-shaped cookie cutter. Place cutouts on prepared cookie sheets. Repeat with chocolate dough.

4. Use smaller heart-shaped cookie cutter to remove small section from centers of hearts. Place small peanut butter hearts into large chocolate hearts; place small chocolate hearts into large peanut butter hearts. Press together lightly.

5. Bake 12 to 14 minutes or until edges are lightly browned. Remove to wire racks; cool completely. *Makes 4 dozen cookies*

Chocolate Cookie Dough

  1 **cup (2 sticks) butter, softened**
  1 **cup sugar**
  1 **egg**
  1 **teaspoon vanilla**
  2 **ounces semisweet chocolate, melted**
2¼ **cups all-purpose flour**
  1 **teaspoon baking powder**
 ¼ **teaspoon salt**

1. Beat butter and sugar in large bowl at high speed of electric mixer until fluffy. Beat in egg and vanilla. Add melted chocolate; mix well.

2. Add flour, baking powder and salt; mix well. Cover; refrigerate about 2 hours or until firm.

May your home be filled with interesting food and delicious conversation.

Valentine Stained Glass Hearts

½ **cup butter or margarine, softened**
¾ **cup granulated sugar**
2 **eggs**
1 **teaspoon vanilla extract**
2⅓ **cups all-purpose flour**
1 **teaspoon baking powder**
  Red hard candies, crushed (about ⅓ cup)
  Frosting (optional)

Cream butter and sugar in mixing bowl. Beat in eggs and vanilla. Sift flour and baking powder together. Gradually stir in flour mixture until dough is very stiff. Cover and chill. Dough needs to chill 3 hours to overnight.

Preheat oven to 375°F. Roll out dough to ⅛-inch thickness on lightly floured surface. To prevent cookies from becoming tough and brittle, do not incorporate too much flour. Cut out cookies using large heart-shaped cookie cutter or use sharp knife and cut heart design. Transfer cookies to foil-lined baking sheet. Using small heart-shaped cookie cutter, cut out and remove heart design from center of each cookie. Fill cutout sections with crushed candy. Bake 7 to 9 minutes or until cookies are lightly browned and candy has melted. Do not overcook.

Remove from oven; immediately slide foil off baking sheet. Cool completely; carefully loosen cookies from foil. If desired, pipe decorative borders with frosting around edges.

Makes about 2½ dozen medium cookies

Favorite recipe from **The Sugar Association, Inc.**

Spicy Gingerbread Cookies

Cookies
- ½ **cup packed brown sugar**
- ¾ **cup (1½ sticks) butter, softened**
- ⅔ **cup light molasses**
- 1 **egg**
- 1½ **teaspoons grated lemon peel**
- 2½ **cups all-purpose flour**
- 1¼ **teaspoons ground cinnamon**
- 1 **teaspoon ground allspice**
- 1 **teaspoon vanilla**
- ½ **teaspoon salt**
- ½ **teaspoon baking soda**
- ½ **teaspoon ground ginger**
- ¼ **teaspoon baking powder**

Frosting
- 4 **cups powdered sugar**
- ½ **cup (1 stick) butter, softened**
- 4 **tablespoons milk**
- 2 **teaspoons vanilla**
- **Assorted food colors (optional)**

1. For cookies, combine brown sugar, butter, molasses, egg and lemon peel in large bowl. Beat at medium speed of electric mixer until smooth and creamy. Add all remaining cookie ingredients. Reduce speed to low; beat well. Cover; refrigerate at least 2 hours.

2. Preheat oven to 350°F. Grease cookie sheets; set aside. Roll out dough, one half at a time, on well floured surface to ¼-inch thickness. (Keep remaining dough refrigerated.) Cut with 3- to 4-inch cookie cutters. Place on prepared cookie sheets. Bake 6 to 8 minutes or until no indentation remains when touched. Remove immediately. Cool completely.

3. For frosting, combine powdered sugar, butter, milk and vanilla in small bowl. Beat at low speed until fluffy. Tint frosting with food colors, if desired. Decorate cookies with frosting.

Makes about 4 dozen cookies

Philadelphia® Sugar Cookies

Prep Time: 10 minutes plus refrigerating
Bake Time: 15 minutes

    1 **package (8 ounces) PHILADELPHIA® Cream Cheese,**
       softened
    1 **cup (2 sticks) butter or margarine, softened**
    ⅔ **cup sugar**
    ¼ **teaspoon vanilla**
    2 **cups flour**
      Colored sugar, sprinkles and colored gels

BEAT cream cheese, butter, ⅔ cup sugar and vanilla with electric mixer on medium speed until well blended. Mix in flour. Refrigerate several hours or overnight.

ROLL dough to ¼-inch thickness on lightly floured surface. Cut into desired shapes; sprinkle with colored sugar. Place on *ungreased* cookie sheets.

BAKE at 350°F for 12 to 15 minutes or until edges are lightly browned. Cool on wire racks. Decorate as desired with colored sugar, sprinkles and colored gels. *Makes 3½ dozen*

Classic Cutouts

Kringle's Cutouts

⅔ Butter Flavor CRISCO® Stick or ⅔ cup Butter Flavor
    CRISCO® all-vegetable shortening
¾ cup sugar
1 tablespoon plus 1 teaspoon milk
1 teaspoon vanilla
1 egg
2 cups all-purpose flour
1½ teaspoons baking powder
¼ teaspoon salt

1. Cream shortening, sugar, milk and vanilla in large bowl at medium speed of electric mixer until well blended. Beat in egg. Combine flour, baking powder and salt. Mix into creamed mixture. Cover; refrigerate several hours or overnight.

2. Heat oven to 375°F. Place sheets of foil on countertop for cooling cookies.

3. Roll dough, half at a time, to ⅛-inch thickness on floured surface. Cut into desired shapes. Place cookies 2 inches apart on *ungreased* cookie sheet. Sprinkle with colored sugar and decors, or leave plain to frost when cool.

4. Bake at 375°F for 7 to 9 minutes. *Do not overbake.* Cool 2 minutes on baking sheet. Remove cookies to foil to cool completely.

Makes about 3 dozen cookies

Cook's Tip: Floured pastry cloth and rolling pin cover make rolling out dough easier.

Gingerbread Folks

1 recipe Gingerbread Cookie dough (recipe follows)
Assorted food colors
Vanilla frosting and assorted decorating gels
Assorted candies and decorations

Supplies
6-inch gingerbread boy and girl cookie cutters

1. Preheat oven to 350°F. Grease cookie sheets.

2. Roll dough on floured surface to ⅛-inch thickness. Cut out dough with cookie cutters. Place on prepared cookie sheets. Bend arms and legs to make cookies look like they're dancing.

3. Bake 8 to 10 minutes or until edges begin to brown. Remove to wire racks; cool completely.

4. Color frosting and decorate as desired.

Makes about 6 large cookies

Gingerbread Cookie Dough

  ½ **cup shortening**
  ⅓ **cup packed light brown sugar**
  ¼ **cup dark molasses**
  1 **egg white**
  ½ **teaspoon vanilla**
1½ **cups all-purpose flour**
  ½ **teaspoon baking soda**
  ½ **teaspoon salt**
  ¼ **teaspoon baking powder**
  1 **teaspoon ground cinnamon**
  ½ **teaspoon ground ginger**

1. Beat shortening, brown sugar, molasses, egg white and vanilla in large bowl at high speed of electric mixer until smooth. Combine flour, baking soda, salt, baking powder and spices in small bowl.

Add to shortening mixture; mix well. Cover; refrigerate until firm, about 8 hours or overnight.

2. Preheat oven to 350°F. Grease cookie sheets.

3. Roll dough on floured surface to ⅛-inch thickness. Cut into desired shapes with cookie cutters. Place on prepared cookie sheets.

4. Bake 6 to 8 minutes or until edges begin to brown. Remove to wire racks; cool completely.   *Makes about 2½ dozen cookies*

Butter Cookies

> ¾ **cup (1½ sticks) butter, softened**
> ¼ **cup granulated sugar**
> ¼ **cup packed light brown sugar**
> 1 **egg yolk**
> 1¾ **cups all-purpose flour**
> ¾ **teaspoon baking powder**
> ⅛ **teaspoon salt**

1. Combine butter, sugars and egg yolk in medium bowl. Add flour, baking powder and salt; mix well. Cover; refrigerate until firm, about 4 hours or overnight.

2. Preheat oven to 350°F.

3. Roll dough on lightly floured surface to ¼-inch thickness; cut into desired shapes with cookie cutters. Place on *ungreased* cookie sheets.

4. Bake 8 to 10 minutes or until edges begin to brown. Remove to wire racks; cool completely.   *Makes about 2 dozen cookies*

Christmas Sugar Cookies

Prep Time: 20 minutes
Chill Time: 1 hour
Bake Time: 12 minutes

1 cup DOMINO® Granulated Sugar
¾ cup butter or margarine, softened
1 egg
1 teaspoon grated lemon peel
1 teaspoon vanilla
¼ teaspoon lemon extract
3 cups all-purpose flour
1 teaspoon baking powder
½ teaspoon salt
Assorted Christmas candies and sprinkles

Cream sugar and butter in large bowl until light and fluffy. Add egg, lemon peel, vanilla and lemon extract; mix well. Add flour, baking powder and salt, beating at low speed until well mixed. Refrigerate dough 1 hour or until chilled.

Heat oven to 350°F. On well floured surface, roll out half of dough to ⅛-inch thickness. Cut with cookie cutters; place on *ungreased* cookie sheets. Decorate with candies and sprinkles. Repeat with remaining half of dough. Bake 9 to 12 minutes or until lightly browned at edges.

Makes about 3 dozen (3-inch) cookies

Frosted Holiday Cut-Outs

1¼ cups granulated sugar
1 Butter Flavor CRISCO® Stick or 1 cup Butter Flavor
   CRISCO® all-vegetable shortening
2 eggs
¼ cup light corn syrup or regular pancake syrup
1 tablespoon vanilla
3 cups plus 4 tablespoons all-purpose flour, divided
¾ teaspoon baking powder
½ teaspoon baking soda
½ teaspoon salt

Icing
1 cup confectioners' sugar
2 tablespoons milk
   Food color (optional)
   Decorating icing

1. Combine sugar and shortening in large bowl. Beat at medium speed of electric mixer until well blended. Add eggs, syrup and vanilla; beat until well blended and fluffy. Combine 3 cups flour, baking powder, baking soda and salt in medium bowl. Gradually add to shortening mixture, beating at low speed until well blended. Divide dough into 4 equal pieces; shape each into disk. Wrap with plastic wrap. Refrigerate 1 hour or until firm.

2. Heat oven to 375°F. Place sheets of foil on countertop for cooling cookies. Sprinkle about 1 tablespoon flour on large sheet of waxed paper. Place disk of dough on floured paper; flatten slightly with hands. Turn dough over; cover with another large sheet of waxed paper. Roll dough to ¼-inch thickness. Remove top sheet of waxed paper. Cut into shapes with floured cookie cutters. Place 2 inches apart on *ungreased* baking sheet. Repeat with remaining dough.

3. Bake one baking sheet at a time at 375°F for 5 to 7 minutes or until edges of cookies are lightly browned. *Do not overbake.* Cool 2 minutes on baking sheet. Remove cookies to foil to cool completely.

4. For icing, combine confectioners' sugar and milk; stir until smooth. Add food color, if desired. Stir until blended. Spread icing on cookies; place on foil until icing is set.   *Makes about 3½ dozen cookies*

Old-World Traditions

Kolacky

½ cup (1 stick) butter or margarine, softened
3 ounces cream cheese, softened
1 teaspoon vanilla
1 cup all-purpose flour
⅛ teaspoon salt
½ cup all-fruit spread, assorted flavors
1 egg
1 teaspoon cold water

1. Combine butter and cream cheese in large bowl; beat with electric mixer at medium speed until smooth and creamy. Beat in vanilla. Combine flour and salt in small bowl; gradually add to margarine mixture, beating until mixture forms soft dough. Divide dough in half; wrap each half in plastic wrap. Refrigerate until firm.

2. Preheat oven to 375°F.

3. Roll out half of dough on lightly floured pastry cloth or board to ⅛-inch thickness. Cut into 3-inch squares. Beat egg with water in small bowl; lightly brush onto dough squares. Spoon 1 teaspoon fruit spread onto center of each square. Bring two edges of dough up over fruit spread; pinch edges together to seal. Place on *ungreased* cookie sheets; brush with egg mixture. Repeat with remaining dough and fruit spread.

4. Bake 12 minutes or until golden brown. Let stand on cookie sheets 1 minute. Transfer cookies to wire racks; cool completely. Store in tightly covered container.

Makes 2 dozen kolacky

Belgian Tuile Cookies

½ **cup (1 stick) butter, softened**
½ **cup sugar**
 1 **egg white**
 1 **teaspoon vanilla**
¼ **teaspoon salt**
½ **cup all-purpose flour**
 4 **ounces bittersweet chocolate, chopped or semisweet
    chocolate chips**

1. Preheat oven to 375°F. Grease cookie sheets; set aside.

2. Beat butter and sugar in large bowl until light and fluffy. Beat in egg white, vanilla and salt. Gradually add flour. Beat until well blended. Drop rounded teaspoonfuls of batter 4 inches apart onto prepared cookie sheets. (Bake only 4 cookies per sheet.) Flatten slightly with spatula.

3. Bake 6 to 8 minutes or until cookies are deep golden brown. Let cookies stand on cookie sheet 1 minute. Working quickly, while cookies are still hot, drape cookies over rolling pin or bottle so both sides hang down and form saddle shape; cool completely.

4. Melt chocolate in small heavy saucepan over low heat, stirring constantly.

5. Tilt saucepan to pool chocolate at one end; dip edge of each cookie, turning slowly so entire edge is tinged with chocolate.

6. Transfer cookies to waxed paper; let stand at room temperature 1 hour or until set. Store tightly covered at room temperature. *Do not freeze.*   *Makes about 2½ dozen cookies*

Berlinerkranser (Little Wreaths)

 1 **Butter Flavor CRISCO® Stick or 1 cup Butter Flavor CRISCO® all-vegetable shortening**
 1 **cup confectioners' sugar**
 2 **large hard boiled egg yolks, mashed**
 2 **large eggs, separated**
 1 **teaspoon vanilla**
 1 **teaspoon almond extract**
2¼ **cups all-purpose flour**
    Green colored sugar crystals
 12 **red candied cherries, cut into quarters**

1. Combine shortening and confectioners' sugar in large bowl. Beat on medium speed with electric mixer until well blended. Beat in hard boiled egg yolks, uncooked egg yolks, vanilla and almond extract. Beat in flour, ¼ cup at a time, until well blended. Cover and refrigerate 3 hours.

2. Let dough stand at room temperature until it becomes easy to handle.

3. Heat oven to 350°F. Divide dough into 2 equal portions. Cut each portion into 24 equal pieces. Roll each piece of dough into 5-inch long rope. Form each rope into wreath or loop 1½ inches apart on *ungreased* cookie sheet, overlapping both ends. Brush each wreath with beaten egg white; sprinkle with colored sugar crystals. Lightly press cherry piece into top of each wreath.

4. Bake at 350°F for 10 to 12 minutes or until edges are lightly browned. Cool on cookie sheets 3 minutes; transfer to cooling racks.

Makes about 4 dozen cookies

Note: These wreath shaped cookies are a Norwegian holiday favorite for the family to bake together.

Viennese Hazelnut Butter Thins

(Pictured on page 185)

    1 cup hazelnuts
 1¼ cups all-purpose flour
  ¼ teaspoon salt
 1¼ cups powdered sugar
    1 cup (2 sticks) butter, softened
    1 egg
    1 teaspoon vanilla
    1 cup semisweet chocolate chips

1. Preheat oven to 350°F. To remove skins from hazelnuts, spread in single layer on baking sheet. Bake 10 to 12 minutes or until toasted and skins begin to flake off; let cool slightly. Wrap hazelnuts in heavy kitchen towel; rub against towel to remove as much of the skins as possible.

2. Place hazelnuts in food processor. Process using on/off pulsing action until hazelnuts are ground but not pasty.

3. Combine flour and salt in small bowl. Beat powdered sugar and butter in medium bowl with electric mixer at medium speed until light and fluffy. Beat in egg and vanilla. Gradually add flour mixture. Beat in ground hazelnuts at low speed until well blended.

4. Place dough on sheet of waxed paper. Using waxed paper to hold dough, roll back and forth to form log 12 inches long and 2½ inches wide. Wrap log in plastic wrap; refrigerate until firm, at least 2 hours or up to 48 hours.

5. Preheat oven to 350°F. Cut dough into ¼-inch-thick slices; place on *ungreased* cookie sheets.

6. Bake 10 to 12 minutes or until edges are very lightly browned. Let cookies stand on cookie sheets 1 minute. Remove cookies to wire racks; cool completely.

7. Place chocolate chips in 2-cup glass measure. Microwave at HIGH 1 to 1½ minutes or until melted, stirring after 1 minute and at 30-second intervals after first minute.

8. Dip cookies into chocolate, coating about ½ of each cookie, let excess drip back into cup or spread chocolate on cookies with a narrow spatula. Transfer cookies to waxed paper; let stand at room temperature 1 hour or until set.   *Makes about 3 dozen cookies*

Cook's Tip: To store cookies, place in airtight container between layers of waxed paper. Cookies can be frozen for up to 3 months.

Chocolate Spritz

   2 squares (1 ounce each) unsweetened chocolate
   1 cup (2 sticks) butter, softened
   ½ cup granulated sugar
   1 egg
   1 teaspoon vanilla
   ¼ teaspoon salt
  2¼ cups all-purpose flour
      Powdered sugar

Preheat oven to 400°F. Line cookie sheets with parchment paper or leave *ungreased*. Melt chocolate in top of double boiler over hot, not boiling, water. Remove from heat; cool. Beat butter, granulated sugar, egg, vanilla and salt in large bowl until light. Blend in melted chocolate and flour until stiff. Fit cookie press with your choice of plate. Load press with dough; press cookies out onto cookie sheets, spacing 2 inches apart.

Bake 5 to 7 minutes or just until very slightly browned around edges. Remove to wire racks to cool. Sprinkle with powdered sugar.
                                                        Makes about 5 dozen cookies

Bavarian Cookie Wreaths

3½ **cups unsifted all-purpose flour**
1 **cup sugar, divided**
3 **teaspoons grated orange peel, divided**
¼ **teaspoon salt**
1⅓ **cups butter or margarine**
¼ **cup Florida orange juice**
⅓ **cup finely chopped blanched almonds**
1 **egg white beaten with 1 teaspoon water**
  Prepared frosting (optional)

Preheat oven to 400°F. In large bowl, mix flour, ¾ cup sugar, 2 teaspoons orange peel and salt. Using pastry blender, cut in butter and orange juice until mixture holds together. Knead a few times and press into a ball.

Shape dough into ¾-inch balls; lightly roll each ball on floured board into a 6-inch-long strip. Using two strips, twist together to make a rope. Pinch ends of rope together to make a wreath; place on lightly greased baking sheet.

In shallow dish, mix almonds, remaining ¼ cup sugar and 1 teaspoon orange peel. Brush top of each wreath with egg white mixture and sprinkle with sugar-almond mixture.

Bake 8 to 10 minutes or until lightly browned. Remove to wire racks; cool completely. Frost, if desired.   *Makes 5 dozen cookies*

Favorite recipe from **Florida Department of Citrus**

Christmas Spritz Cookies

2¼ cups all-purpose flour
¼ teaspoon salt
1¼ cups powdered sugar
1 cup (2 sticks) butter, softened
1 egg
1 teaspoon almond extract
1 teaspoon vanilla
Green food coloring (optional)
Candied red and green cherries and assorted decorative candies (optional)
Icing (recipe follows, optional)

1. Preheat oven to 375°F. Place flour and salt in medium bowl; stir to combine. Beat powdered sugar and butter in large bowl until light and fluffy. Beat in egg, almond extract and vanilla. Gradually add flour mixture. Beat until well blended.

2. Divide dough in half. If desired, tint half of dough with green food coloring. Fit cookie press with desired plate (or change plates for different shapes after first batch). Fill press with dough; press dough 1 inch apart onto *ungreased* cookie sheets. Decorate cookies with cherries and assorted candies, if desired.

3. Bake 10 to 12 minutes or until just set. Remove cookies to wire racks; cool completely.

4. Prepare Icing, if desired. Pipe or drizzle on cooled cookies. Decorate with cherries and assorted candies, if desired. Store tightly covered at room temperature or freeze up to 3 months.

Makes about 5 dozen cookies

Icing

1½ cups powdered sugar
2 tablespoons milk plus additional, if needed
⅛ teaspoon almond extract

Place all ingredients in medium bowl; stir until thick, but spreadable. (If icing is too thick, stir in 1 teaspoon additional milk.)

Czech Bear Paws (Medvedi Tlapicvky)

- **4 cups toasted ground hazelnuts**
- **2 cups all-purpose flour**
- **1 tablespoon unsweetened cocoa powder**
- **1 teaspoon ground cinnamon**
- **½ teaspoon ground nutmeg**
- **¼ teaspoon salt**
- **1 cup (2 sticks) plus 3 teaspoons butter, softened, divided**
- **1 cup powdered sugar**
- **1 egg yolk**
- **½ cup chocolate chips, melted**
- **Slivered almonds, halved**

1. Preheat oven to 350°F. Place hazelnuts, flour, cocoa, cinnamon, nutmeg and salt in medium bowl; stir to combine.

2. Beat 1 cup butter, powdered sugar and egg yolk in large bowl with electric mixer at medium speed until light and fluffy. Gradually add flour mixture. Beat at low speed until soft dough forms.

3. Grease 3 madeleine pans with remaining butter, 1 teaspoon per pan; dust with flour. (If only 1 madeleine pan is available, thoroughly wash, dry, regrease and flour after baking each batch. Cover remaining dough with plastic wrap; let stand at room temperature.) Press level tablespoonfuls of dough into each mold.

4. Bake 12 minutes or until lightly browned. Let cookies stand in pan 3 minutes. Carefully loosen cookies from pan with point of small knife. Invert pan over wire rack; tap lightly to release cookies. Let stand 2 minutes. Turn cookies shell-side up; cool completely.

5. Pipe squiggle of melted chocolate on curved end of each cookie; place slivered almond halves in melted chocolate for claws. Let stand at room temperature 1 hour or until set.

6. Store tightly covered at room temperature.

Makes about 5 dozen cookies

Cook's Tip: These cookies do not freeze well.

German Honey Bars (Lebkuchen)

2¾ cups all-purpose flour
  2 teaspoons ground cinnamon
  1 teaspoon baking powder
  ½ teaspoon baking soda
  ½ teaspoon salt
  ½ teaspoon ground cardamom
  ½ teaspoon ground ginger
  ½ cup honey
  ½ cup dark molasses
  ¾ cup packed brown sugar
  3 tablespoons butter, melted
  1 large egg
  ½ cup chopped toasted almonds (optional)
    Glaze (recipe follows)

Preheat oven to 350°F. Grease 15×10-inch jelly-roll pan; set aside. Combine flour, cinnamon, baking powder, baking soda, salt, cardamom and ginger in medium bowl. Combine honey and molasses in medium saucepan; bring to a boil over medium heat. Remove from heat; cool 10 minutes. Stir in brown sugar, butter and egg.

Place brown sugar mixture in large bowl. Gradually add flour mixture. Beat at low speed with electric mixer until dough forms. Stir in almonds with spoon, if desired. (Dough will be slightly sticky.) Spread dough evenly into prepared pan. Bake 20 to 22 minutes or until golden brown and set. Remove pan to wire rack; cool completely.

Prepare Glaze. Spread over cooled bar cookies. Let stand until set, about 30 minutes. Cut into bars. Store tightly covered at room temperature or freeze up to 3 months. *Makes about 6 dozen bars*

Glaze

1¼ cups powdered sugar
  3 tablespoons fresh lemon juice
  1 teaspoon grated lemon peel

Place all ingredients in medium bowl; stir with spoon until smooth.

Fruitcake Slices

    1 cup (2 sticks) butter, softened
    1 cup powdered sugar
    1 egg
    1 teaspoon vanilla
  1½ cups coarsely chopped candied fruit (fruitcake mix)
   ½ cup coarsely chopped walnuts
  2½ cups all-purpose unsifted flour, divided
   ¾ to 1 cup flaked coconut
      Maraschino cherry halves (optional)

1. Beat butter in large bowl with electric mixer at medium speed until smooth. Add powdered sugar; beat until well blended. Add egg and vanilla; beat until well blended.

2. Combine candied fruit and walnuts in medium bowl. Stir in remaining ¼ cup flour into fruit mixture. Add remaining 2¼ cups flour to butter mixture; beat at low speed until blended. Stir into fruit mixture with spoon.

3. Shape dough into 2 logs, each about 2 inches in diameter and 5½ inches long. Spread coconut evenly on sheet of waxed paper. Roll logs in coconut, coating evenly. Wrap each log in plastic wrap. Refrigerate 2 to 3 hours or overnight, or freeze up to 1 month. (Let frozen logs stand at room temperature about 10 minutes before slicing and baking.)

4. Preheat oven to 350°F. Grease cookie sheets. Cut logs into ¼-inch-thick slices; place 1 inch apart on cookie sheets.

5. Bake 13 to 15 minutes or until edges are golden brown. Transfer to wire racks to cool. Decorate with cherry halves, if desired. Store in airtight container. *Makes about 4 dozen cookies*

European Kolacky

1 cup butter or margarine, softened
1 package (8 ounces) cream cheese, softened
1 tablespoon sugar
1 tablespoon milk
1 egg yolk
1½ cups all-purpose flour
½ teaspoon baking powder
1 can SOLO® or 1 jar BAKER® Filling (any flavor)
Powdered sugar

Cream butter, cream cheese, sugar and milk in medium bowl with electric mixer until thoroughly blended. Beat in egg yolk. Sift together flour and baking powder; stir into butter mixture to make stiff dough. Cover and refrigerate several hours or overnight.

Preheat oven to 400°F. Roll out dough on lightly floured surface to ¼-inch thickness. Cut dough with floured 2-inch cookie cutter. Place cookies on *ungreased* cookie sheets about 1 inch apart. Make depression in centers of cookies with thumb or back of spoon. Spoon ½ teaspoon filling into centers of cookies.

Bake 10 to 12 minutes or until lightly browned. Remove from baking sheets and cool completely on wire racks. Sprinkle with powdered sugar just before serving. *Makes about 3 dozen cookies*

Danish Lemon-Filled Spice Cookies
(Medaljekager)

2¼ cups all-purpose flour
1 teaspoon ground cinnamon
½ teaspoon ground allspice
½ teaspoon ground ginger
½ teaspoon ground nutmeg
¼ teaspoon salt
¾ cup (1½ sticks) butter, softened
¾ cup sugar
¼ cup milk
1 egg yolk
1 teaspoon vanilla
Additional sugar
Lemon Filling (recipe page 197)

1. Place flour, cinnamon, allspice, ginger, nutmeg and salt in medium bowl; stir to combine. Beat butter, sugar, milk, egg yolk and vanilla in large bowl. Beat butter mixture with electric mixer at medium speed until light and fluffy. Gradually add flour mixture. Beat at low speed until dough forms. Cover dough and refrigerate 30 minutes or until firm.

2. Preheat oven to 350°F. Grease cookie sheets. Shape teaspoonfuls of dough into ½-inch balls; place 2 inches apart on prepared cookie sheets. Flatten each ball to ¼-inch thickness with bottom of glass dipped in sugar. Prick top of each cookie using fork. Bake 10 to 13 minutes or until golden brown. Remove cookies to wire racks; cool completely.

3. Prepare Lemon Filling. Spread filling on flat side of half of cookies. Top with remaining cookies, pressing flat sides together. Let stand at room temperature until set. Store tightly covered at room temperature or freeze up to 3 months. *Makes about 3 dozen sandwich cookies*

Lemon Filling

2¼ cups sifted powdered sugar
3 tablespoons lemon juice
1½ tablespoons butter, softened
½ teaspoon lemon extract

Beat all ingredients in medium bowl with electric mixer at medium speed until smooth.   *Makes about 1 cup*

Linzer Tarts

1 cup margarine or butter, softened
1 cup granulated sugar
2 cups all-purpose flour
1 cup PLANTERS® Slivered Almonds, chopped
1 teaspoon grated lemon peel
¼ teaspoon ground cinnamon
⅓ cup raspberry preserves
Powdered sugar

1. Beat margarine and sugar in large bowl with electric mixer at high speed until light and fluffy. Stir in flour, almonds, lemon peel and cinnamon until blended. Cover; refrigerate 2 hours.

2. Divide dough in half. Roll out half of dough on floured surface to ⅛-inch thickness. Cut circles from dough using 2½-inch round cookie cutter. Reroll scraps to make additional rounds. Cut out ½-inch circles from centers of half the rounds. Repeat with remaining dough. Place on *ungreased* cookie sheets.

3. Bake at 325°F for 12 to 15 minutes or until lightly browned. Remove from cookie sheets; cool on wire racks. Spread preserves on flat side of whole cookies. Top with cut-out cookies to make sandwiches. Dust with powdered sugar.

Makes about 2 dozen cookies

Raspberry Linzer Rounds

1¼ cups granulated sugar
 1 Butter Flavor CRISCO® Stick or 1 cup Butter Flavor
     CRISCO® all-vegetable shortening
 2 eggs
¼ cup light corn syrup or regular pancake syrup
 1 teaspoon almond extract
 1 teaspoon vanilla
 2 cups plus 4 tablespoons all-purpose flour, divided
 1 cup ground almonds (about 4 to 5 ounces)
¾ teaspoon baking powder
½ teaspoon baking soda
½ teaspoon salt
½ cup seedless SMUCKER'S® Raspberry Preserves, stirred
     Confectioners' sugar

1. Place granulated sugar and shortening in large bowl. Beat at medium speed of electric mixer until well blended. Add eggs, syrup and almond extract and vanilla; beat until blended and fluffy.

2. Combine 2 cups flour, ground almonds, baking powder, baking soda and salt. Add gradually to shortening mixture, beating at low speed until well blended.

3. Divide dough into 4 pieces; shape each piece into disk. Wrap with plastic wrap. Refrigerate several hours or until firm.

4. Heat oven to 375°F. Place sheets of foil on countertop for cooling cookies.

5. Sprinkle about 1 tablespoon flour on large sheet of waxed paper. Place disk of dough on floured paper; flatten slightly with hands. Turn dough over and cover with another large sheet of waxed paper. Roll dough to ¼-inch thickness. Remove top sheet of waxed paper. Cut out with 2- or 2½-inch floured scalloped round cookie cutter. Place 2 inches apart on *ungreased* baking sheet. Repeat with remaining dough. Cut out centers of half the cookies with ½- or ¾-inch round cookie cutter.

6. Bake one baking sheet at a time at 375°F for 5 to 9 minutes or until edges of cookies are lightly browned.* *Do not overbake.* Cool 2 minutes on baking sheet. Remove cookies to foil to cool completely.

7. Spread a small amount of raspberry jam on bottom of solid cookies; cover with cut-out cookies, bottom sides down, to form sandwiches. Sift confectioners' sugar, if desired, over tops of cookies.

Makes about 2 dozen cookies

Bake larger cookies 1 to 2 minutes longer.

Snowballs

>   ½ cup DOMINO® Confectioners 10-X Sugar
>   ¼ teaspoon salt
>   1 cup butter or margarine, softened
>   1 teaspoon vanilla extract
>   2¼ cups all-purpose flour
>   ½ cup chopped pecans
>   DOMINO® Confectioners 10-X Sugar

In large bowl, combine ½ cup confectioners sugar, salt and butter; mix well. Add extract. Gradually stir in flour. Work nuts into dough. Chill well. Form into 1-inch balls. Place on *ungreased* cookie sheets. Bake at 400°F for 8 to 10 minutes or until set but not brown. Roll in confectioners sugar immediately. Cool on rack. Roll in sugar again. Store in airtight container.

Makes 5 dozen cookies

Old-World Traditions

Orange-Cardamom Thins

1¼ cups granulated sugar
  1 Butter Flavor CRISCO® Stick or 1 cup Butter Flavor
     CRISCO® all-vegetable shortening plus additional
     for greasing
  1 egg
 ¼ cup light corn syrup or regular pancake syrup
  1 teaspoon vanilla
  1 tablespoon grated orange peel
 ½ teaspoon orange extract
  3 cups all-purpose flour
1¼ teaspoons cardamom
 ¾ teaspoon baking powder
 ½ teaspoon baking soda
 ½ teaspoon salt
 ½ teaspoon cinnamon

1. Place sugar and shortening in large bowl. Beat at medium speed of electric mixer until well blended. Add egg, syrup, vanilla, orange peel and orange extract; beat until well blended and fluffy.

2. Combine flour, cardamom, baking powder, baking soda, salt and cinnamon. Add gradually to shortening mixture, beating at low speed until well blended.

3. Divide dough in half. Roll each half into 12-inch-long log. Wrap with plastic wrap. Refrigerate for 4 hours or until firm.

4. Heat oven to 375°F. Grease baking sheets with shortening. Place sheets of foil on countertop for cooling cookies.

5. Cut rolls into ¼-inch-thick slices. Place 1 inch apart on prepared baking sheets.

6. Bake one baking sheet at a time at 375°F for 7 to 9 minutes or until bottoms of cookies are lightly browned. *Do not overbake.* Cool 2 minutes on baking sheet. Remove cookies to foil to cool completely.
Makes about 8 dozen cookies

Rugelach

Prep Time: 1 hour plus refrigerating
Bake Time: 22 minutes

　　1　package (8 ounces) PHILADELPHIA® Cream Cheese,
　　　　　softened
1¼　cups (2½ sticks) butter or margarine, divided
2¼　cups flour
　　1　cup finely chopped PLANTERS® Walnuts *or* Pecans
　½　cup sugar
　　3　teaspoons ground cinnamon, divided
　　　　Raspberry *or* apricot preserves (optional)
　　2　tablespoons sugar

MIX cream cheese and 1 cup of the butter with electric mixer on medium speed until well blended. Gradually add flour, mixing until blended. (Dough will be very soft and sticky.) Divide dough into 4 portions; place each on sheet of plastic wrap. Shape each portion into 1-inch-thick circle, using floured hands. Wrap plastic wrap around each circle to enclose. Refrigerate overnight.

LINE greased cookie sheets with foil or parchment paper. Roll each portion of dough to 11-inch circle on lightly floured surface, lifting dough occasionally to add additional flour to surface to prevent sticking. Melt remaining ¼ cup butter. Mix walnuts, ½ cup sugar and 2 teaspoons of the cinnamon. Melt remaining ¼ cup margarine; brush onto dough. Sprinkle evenly with walnut mixture.

CUT each circle into 16 wedges. Spoon ¼ teaspoon preserves at wide end of each wedge; roll up, starting at wide end. Place, point sides down, on prepared cookie sheets. Brush tops lightly with additional melted butter; sprinkle with combined remaining 1 teaspoon cinnamon and 2 tablespoons sugar.

BAKE at 350°F for 19 to 22 minutes or until lightly browned. Remove immediately from cookie sheet. Cool on wire racks.

Makes about 5 dozen cookies

Snowball Cookies

Prep Time: 15 minutes
Chill Time: 1 hour
Cook Time: 10 minutes
Total Time: 1 hour and 25 minutes

> **1 cup margarine or butter, softened**
> **1 cup sugar**
> **1 teaspoon vanilla extract**
> **2 cups all-purpose flour**
> **1½ cups PLANTERS® Pecans, finely ground**
> **¼ teaspoon salt**
> **½ cup powdered sugar**

1. Beat margarine or butter, sugar and vanilla in large bowl with mixer at medium speed until creamy. Blend in flour, pecans and salt. Refrigerate 1 hour.

2. Shape dough into 1-inch balls. Place on *ungreased* baking sheets, 2 inches apart. Bake in preheated 350°F oven for 10 to 12 minutes. Remove from sheets; cool on wire racks. Dust with powdered sugar. Store in airtight container.   *Makes 6 dozen cookies*

Swedish Spritz

1 **Butter Flavor CRISCO® Stick or ½ cup Butter Flavor**
  CRISCO® all-vegetable shortening
1 **cup granulated sugar**
1 **egg**
1 **tablespoon milk**
1 **teaspoon almond extract**
2 **cups all-purpose flour**
½ **cup finely ground blanched almonds**
¼ **teaspoon salt**
⅛ **teaspoon baking powder**
  Colored sugar crystals (optional)

1. Heat oven to 350°F. Refrigerate *ungreased* baking sheets. Place sheets of foil on countertop for cooling cookies.

2. Combine shortening and granulated sugar in large bowl. Beat at medium speed of electric mixer until well blended. Beat in egg, milk and almond extract.

3. Combine flour, nuts, salt and baking powder. Add gradually to creamed mixture at low speed. Beat until well blended.

4. Fit cookie press or pastry bag with desired disk or tip. Fill with dough. Press dough out onto cold baking sheet, forming cookies about 1½ inches apart. (Refrigerate dough about 5 minutes or until firm enough to hold its shape if it becomes too soft.) Sprinkle with colored sugar (if used).

5. Bake at 350°F for 8 to 10 minutes or until bottoms are light brown. *Do not overbake.* Cool 2 minutes on baking sheet. Remove cookies to foil to cool completely.   *Makes about 8 dozen cookies*

Vanilkove Rohlicky (Vanilla Crescents)

½ **Butter Flavor CRISCO® Stick or ½ cup Butter Flavor
CRISCO® all-vegetable shortening**
½ **cup granulated sugar**
2 **cups all-purpose flour**
1½ **cups ground almonds**
1 **teaspoon vanilla**
¼ **teaspoon ground allspice**
¼ **teaspoon salt**
Confectioners' sugar

1. Combine shortening and granulated sugar in large bowl. Beat at medium speed with electric mixer until well blended. Beat in flour, ½ cup at a time. Beat in almonds, vanilla, allspice and salt until well blended. Continue to beat until dough is just stiff. Shape dough into ball. Wrap in plastic wrap and refrigerate 2 hours.

2. Heat oven to 350°F. Spray cookie sheets with CRISCO® No-Stick Cooking Spray; set aside.

3. Pinch off round pieces of dough about 1½ inches in diameter. Roll each piece of dough, on floured surface, into 2½×1-inch log. Shape into crescent; place on cookie sheets about 1 inch apart.

4. Bake at 350°F for 15 to 18 minutes or until lightly brown. Cool on cookie sheets 4 minutes; transfer to cooling racks. Dust with confectioners' sugar.   *Makes about 3 dozen cookies*

Viennese Meringue Bars

   1 cup (2 sticks) butter, softened
1¼ cups sugar, divided
   2 egg yolks
   ¼ teaspoon salt
2¼ cups all-purpose flour
   1 cup seedless raspberry jam
1½ cups mini semisweet chocolate chips
   3 egg whites
   ½ cup slivered almonds, toasted

1. Preheat oven to 350°F. Beat butter and ½ cup sugar in large bowl with electric mixer at medium speed until light and fluffy. Beat in egg yolks and salt. Gradually add flour. Beat at low speed until well blended.

2. With buttered fingers, pat dough evenly into *ungreased* 15×10-inch jelly-roll pan. Bake 22 to 25 minutes or until light golden brown. Remove from oven; immediately spread jam over crust. Sprinkle evenly with chocolate chips.

3. For meringue topping, beat egg whites in clean large bowl with electric mixer at high speed until foamy. Gradually beat in remaining ¾ cup sugar until stiff peaks form. Gently stir in almonds with rubber spatula.

4. Spoon meringue over chocolate mixture; spread evenly with small spatula. Bake 20 to 25 minutes or until golden brown. Cool completely on wire rack. Cut into bars. *Makes 28 bars*

Welsh Tea Cakes

¾ **cup chopped dried mixed fruit or fruit bits or golden raisins**
2 **tablespoons brandy or cognac**
2¼ **cups all-purpose flour**
2½ **teaspoons ground cinnamon, divided**
1 **teaspoon baking powder**
½ **teaspoon baking soda**
¼ **teaspoon salt**
¼ **teaspoon ground cloves**
1 **cup (2 sticks) butter, softened**
1¼ **cups sugar, divided**
1 **egg**
⅓ **cup sliced almonds (optional)**

1. Preheat oven to 375°F. Combine dried fruit and brandy in medium bowl; let sit at least 10 minutes to plump.

2. Place flour, 1½ teaspoons cinnamon, baking powder, baking soda, salt and cloves in medium bowl; stir to combine.

3. Beat butter and 1 cup sugar in large bowl until light and fluffy. Beat in egg. Gradually add flour mixture. Beat until well blended. Stir in fruit and brandy mixture with spoon.

4. Combine remaining ¼ cup sugar and 1 teaspoon cinnamon in small bowl. Shape heaping teaspoonfuls of dough into 1-inch balls; roll balls in cinnamon-sugar to coat. Place balls 2 inches apart on *ungreased* cookie sheets.

5. Press balls to ¼-inch thickness using bottom of glass dipped in granulated sugar. Press 3 almond slices horizontally into center of each cookie, if desired. (Almonds will spread evenly and flatten upon baking.)

6. Bake 10 to 12 minutes or until lightly browned. Remove tea cakes to wire racks; cool completely. Store tightly covered at room temperature or freeze up to 3 months.

Makes about 3½ dozen cookies

Danish Raspberry Ribbons

  1 cup (2 sticks) butter, softened
  ½ cup granulated sugar
  1 large egg
  2 tablespoons milk
  2 tablespoons vanilla
  ¼ teaspoon almond extract
  2⅔ cups all-purpose flour
  6 tablespoons seedless raspberry jam
   Glaze (recipe follows)

1. Beat butter and sugar in bowl with electric mixer until light and fluffy. Beat in egg, milk, vanilla and almond extract until well blended.

2. Gradually add 1½ cups flour. Beat at low speed until well blended. Stir in enough remaining flour with spoon to form stiff dough. Form dough into disc; wrap in plastic wrap and refrigerate until firm, at least 30 minutes or overnight.

3. Preheat oven to 375°F. Cut dough into 6 equal pieces. Rewrap 3 dough pieces and return to refrigerator. With floured hands, shape each piece of dough into 12-inch-long, ¾-inch-thick rope.

4. Place ropes 2 inches apart on *ungreased* cookie sheets. Make lengthwise ¼-inch-deep groove down center of each rope with handle of wooden spoon or finger. (Ropes will flatten to ½-inch-thick strips.)

5. Bake 12 minutes. Remove from oven; spoon 1 tablespoon jam into each groove. Return to oven; bake 5 to 7 minutes longer or until strips are light golden brown. Cool strips 15 minutes on cookie sheet.

6. Prepare Glaze. Drizzle strips with Glaze; let stand 5 minutes to dry. Cut cookie strips at 45° angle into 1-inch slices. Place cookies on wire racks. Repeat with remaining dough.   *Makes 5½ dozen cookies*

Glaze: Place ½ cup powdered sugar, 1 tablespoon milk and 1 teaspoon vanilla in small bowl; stir with spoon until smooth. Makes about ¼ cup glaze.

Dutch St. Nicolas Cookies

½ cup whole natural almonds
¾ cup butter or margarine, softened
½ cup packed brown sugar
2 tablespoons milk
1½ teaspoons ground cinnamon
¼ teaspoon ground nutmeg
¼ teaspoon ground ginger
¼ teaspoon ground cloves
2 cups sifted all-purpose flour
1½ teaspoons baking powder
½ teaspoon salt
¼ cup coarsely chopped citron

Spread almonds in single layer on baking sheet. Bake at 375°F, 10 to 12 minutes, stirring occasionally, until lightly toasted. Cool. Chop finely. In large bowl, cream butter, sugar, milk and spices. In small bowl, combine flour, baking powder and salt. Add flour mixture to creamed mixture; blend well. Stir in almonds and citron. Knead dough slightly to make ball. Cover; refrigerate until firm. Roll out dough ¼ inch thick on lightly floured surface. Cut out with cookie cutters. Place 2 inches apart on greased cookie sheets. Bake at 375°F, 7 to 10 minutes, until lightly browned. Remove to wire racks to cool.

Makes about 3½ dozen cookies

Favorite recipe from **Almond Board of California**

Finnish Spice Cookies (Nissu Nassu)

        2 cups all-purpose flour
     1½ teaspoons ground ginger
     1½ teaspoons ground cinnamon
        ½ teaspoon ground cardamom
        ½ teaspoon ground cloves
        ⅔ cup packed light brown sugar
        ½ cup (1 stick) butter, softened
        ½ teaspoon baking soda
        3 to 5 tablespoons hot water
           Royal Icing (recipe page 210)

1. Place flour, ginger, cinnamon, cardamom and cloves in medium bowl; stir to combine.

2. Beat brown sugar and butter in large bowl until light and fluffy. Dissolve baking soda in 3 tablespoons water in cup. Beat into butter mixture. Gradually add flour mixture. Beat until dough forms. (If dough is too crumbly, add more water, 1 tablespoon at a time, until dough holds together.) Form dough into 2 discs; wrap in plastic wrap and refrigerate until firm, 30 minutes or overnight.

3. Preheat oven to 375°F. Grease cookie sheets; set aside.

4. Working with 1 disc at a time, roll out dough on lightly floured surface to ⅛-inch thickness. Cut dough with floured 3-inch pig-shaped cookie cutter or desired cookie cutter. Place cutouts 1 inch apart on prepared cookie sheets. Gently press dough trimmings together; reroll and cut out more cookies.

5. Bake 8 to 10 minutes or until firm and lightly browned. Remove cookies to wire racks; cool completely.

6. Prepare Royal Icing. Spoon icing into pastry bag fitted with writing tip. Decorate cooled cookies with icing. Let stand at room temperature 1 hour or until set. Store tightly covered at room temperature or freeze up to 3 months.

Makes about 5 dozen cookies

Royal Icing

1 egg white,* at room temperature
2 to 2½ cups sifted powdered sugar
½ teaspoon almond extract

*Use only Grade A clean, uncracked egg.

1. Beat egg white in small bowl at high speed of electric mixer until foamy.

2. Gradually add 2 cups powdered sugar and almond extract. Beat at low speed until moistened. Increase mixer speed to high and beat until icing is stiff.   *Makes about 2½ cups*

Mexican Wedding Cookies

1 cup pecan pieces or halves
1 cup (2 sticks) butter, softened
2 cups powdered sugar, divided
2 cups all-purpose flour, divided
2 teaspoons vanilla
⅛ teaspoon salt

1. Place pecans in food processor. Process using on/off pulsing action until pecans are ground but not pasty.

2. Beat butter and ½ cup powdered sugar in large bowl with electric mixer at medium speed until light and fluffy. Gradually add 1 cup flour, vanilla and salt. Beat at low speed until well blended. Stir in remaining 1 cup flour and ground nuts with spoon. Shape dough into ball; wrap in plastic wrap and refrigerate 1 hour or until firm.

3. Preheat oven to 350°F. Shape tablespoons of dough into 1-inch balls. Place 1 inch apart on *ungreased* cookie sheets.

4. Bake 12 to 15 minutes or until pale golden brown. Let cookies stand on cookie sheets 2 minutes.

5. Meanwhile, place 1 cup powdered sugar in 13×9-inch glass dish. Transfer hot cookies to powdered sugar. Roll cookies in powdered sugar, coating well. Let cookies cool in sugar.

6. Sift remaining ½ cup powdered sugar over sugar-coated cookies before serving. Store tightly covered at room temperature or freeze up to 1 month.   *Makes about 4 dozen cookies*

Golden Kolacky

½ **cup (1 stick) butter, softened**
4 **ounces cream cheese, softened**
1 **cup all-purpose flour**
   Fruit preserves

1. Combine butter and cream cheese in large bowl; beat until smooth. Gradually add flour to butter mixture, blending until mixture forms soft dough. Divide dough in half; wrap each half in plastic wrap. Refrigerate until firm.

2. Preheat oven to 375°F. Roll out dough, half at a time, on floured surface to ⅛-inch thickness. Cut into 3-inch squares. Spoon 1 teaspoon preserves into center of each square. Bring up two opposite corners to center; pinch together tightly to seal. Fold sealed tip to one side; pinch to seal.

3. Place 1 inch apart on *ungreased* cookie sheets. Bake 10 to 15 minutes or until lightly browned. Remove to wire racks; cool completely.

Makes about 2½ dozen cookies

A sip. A bite. A reverie.

Molded Scotch Shortbread

1½ **cups all-purpose flour**
¼ **teaspoon salt**
¾ **cup (1½ sticks) butter, softened**
⅓ **cup sugar**
 1 **egg**

1. Preheat oven to temperature recommended by shortbread mold manufacturer. Combine flour and salt in medium bowl.

2. Beat butter and sugar in large bowl with electric mixer at medium speed until light and fluffy. Beat in egg. Gradually add flour mixture. Beat at low speed until well blended.

3. Spray 10-inch ceramic shortbread mold with nonstick cooking spray. Press dough firmly into mold. Bake, cool and remove from mold according to manufacturer's directions.

Makes 1 shortbread mold

Variation: If mold is not available, preheat oven to 350°F. Shape tablespoonfuls of dough into 1-inch balls. Place 2 inches apart on *ungreased* cookie sheets; press with fork to flatten. Bake 18 to 20 minutes or until edges are lightly browned. Let cookies stand on cookie sheets 2 minutes; transfer to wire racks to cool completely. Makes 2 dozen cookies.

Cook's Tip: Butter can be stored in the refrigerator up to 1 month. Be sure to wrap it airtight, as butter readily absorbs flavors and odors from other items in the refrigerator.

Pfeffernüsse

3½ cups all-purpose flour
2 teaspoons baking powder
1½ teaspoons ground cinnamon
1 teaspoon ground ginger
½ teaspoon baking soda
½ teaspoon salt
½ teaspoon ground cloves
½ teaspoon ground cardamom
¼ teaspoon black pepper
1 cup (2 sticks) butter, softened
1 cup granulated sugar
¼ cup dark molasses
1 egg
Powdered sugar

1. Combine flour, baking powder, cinnamon, ginger, baking soda, salt, cloves, cardamom and pepper in large bowl.

2. Beat butter and sugar in large bowl with electric mixer at medium speed until light and fluffy. Beat in molasses and egg. Gradually add flour mixture. Beat at low speed until dough forms. Shape dough into disk; wrap in plastic wrap and refrigerate until firm, 30 minutes or up to 3 days.

3. Preheat oven to 350°F. Grease cookie sheets. Roll dough into 1-inch balls. Place 2 inches apart on prepared cookie sheets.

4. Bake 12 to 14 minutes or until golden brown. Transfer cookies to wire racks; dust with sifted powdered sugar. Cool completely. Store tightly covered at room temperature or freeze up to 3 months.

Makes about 5 dozen cookies

The publisher would like to thank the companies and organizations listed below for the use of their recipes and photographs in this publication.

Almond Board of California
Arm & Hammer Division, Church & Dwight Co., Inc.
Blue Diamond Growers®
Cherry Marketing Institute
ConAgra Foods®
Dole Food Company, Inc.
Domino® Foods, Inc.
Duncan Hines® and Moist Deluxe® are registered trademarks of Aurora Foods Inc.
Eagle® Brand
Florida Department of Citrus
Hershey Foods Corporation
Kellogg Company
Kraft Foods Holdings
Mott's® is a registered trademark of Mott's, Inc.
National Honey Board
Nestlé USA
PLANTERS® Nuts
The Quaker® Oatmeal Kitchens
The J.M. Smucker Company
Sokol and Company
The Sugar Association, Inc.
Sunkist Growers, Inc.
Walnut Marketing Board
Washington Apple Commission
Wisconsin Milk Marketing Board

METRIC CONVERSION CHART

VOLUME MEASUREMENTS (dry)

1/8 teaspoon = 0.5 mL
1/4 teaspoon = 1 mL
1/2 teaspoon = 2 mL
3/4 teaspoon = 4 mL
1 teaspoon = 5 mL
1 tablespoon = 15 mL
2 tablespoons = 30 mL
1/4 cup = 60 mL
1/3 cup = 75 mL
1/2 cup = 125 mL
2/3 cup = 150 mL
3/4 cup = 175 mL
1 cup = 250 mL
2 cups = 1 pint = 500 mL
3 cups = 750 mL
4 cups = 1 quart = 1 L

VOLUME MEASUREMENTS (fluid)

1 fluid ounce (2 tablespoons) = 30 mL
4 fluid ounces (1/2 cup) = 125 mL
8 fluid ounces (1 cup) = 250 mL
12 fluid ounces (1 1/2 cups) = 375 mL
16 fluid ounces (2 cups) = 500 mL

WEIGHTS (mass)

1/2 ounce = 15 g
1 ounce = 30 g
3 ounces = 90 g
4 ounces = 120 g
8 ounces = 225 g
10 ounces = 285 g
12 ounces = 360 g
16 ounces = 1 pound = 450 g

DIMENSIONS

1/16 inch = 2 mm
1/8 inch = 3 mm
1/4 inch = 6 mm
1/2 inch = 1.5 cm
3/4 inch = 2 cm
1 inch = 2.5 cm

OVEN TEMPERATURES

250°F = 120°C
275°F = 140°C
300°F = 150°C
325°F = 160°C
350°F = 180°C
375°F = 190°C
400°F = 200°C
425°F = 220°C
450°F = 230°C

BAKING PAN SIZES

Utensil	Size in Inches/Quarts	Metric Volume	Size in Centimeters
Baking or Cake Pan (square or rectangular)	8×8×2	2 L	20×20×5
	9×9×2	2.5 L	23×23×5
	12×8×2	3 L	30×20×5
	13×9×2	3.5 L	33×23×5
Loaf Pan	8×4×3	1.5 L	20×10×7
	9×5×3	2 L	23×13×7
Round Layer Cake Pan	8×1½	1.2 L	20×4
	9×1½	1.5 L	23×4
Pie Plate	8×1¼	750 mL	20×3
	9×1¼	1 L	23×3
Baking Dish or Casserole	1 quart	1 L	—
	1½ quart	1.5 L	—
	2 quart	2 L	—